MRS THATCHER'S FIRST ADMINISTRATION

MRS THATCHER'S FIRST ADMINISTRATION

The Prophets Confounded

Jock Bruce-Gardyne

M

MACMILLAN

First published 1984 by
THE MACMILLAN PRESS LTD
London and Basingstoke
Companies and representatives
throughout the world

Typeset by
Wessex Typesetters Ltd
Frome, Somerset

Printed in Great Britain by
The Pitman Press,
Bath

British Library Cataloguing in Publication Data
Bruce-Gardyne, Jock
Mrs. Thatcher's first administration.
1. Great Britain—Politics and government
—1979–
I. Title
354.41'0009   JN231
ISBN 0–333–36764–2
ISBN 0–333–37714–1 Pbk

To Roselle, Thomas and Adam

Contents

Preface

Ten years ago I wrote a study of the 1970 Conservative Government, in the aftermath of the February 1974 election, from the viewpoint of a somewhat disillusioned backbencher (*Whatever Happened to the Quiet Revolution?*, Charles Knight, 1974). It was an attempt to analyse how the bid to 'change the course of history of this nation' which Mr Heath had promised us in 1970 had ultimately run into the sands and perished in the conflict with the miners just three-and-a-half years later. Its conclusion was that

> There is nothing to inhibit governments from embarking on a change of course as soon as they assume office: indeed the sooner they do so, the better. What is required of them – and what has been so signally missing in recent years – is a willingness then to wait for results: to recognise that it will be two years before they can begin to see the consequences of their economic choices – and that unless they are prepared to grit their teeth that long they might just as well not embark on a strategy in the first place.

The verdict, in short, was that the 1970 government had been too impatient, and abandoned its intentions before they had had a proper chance; and that its discomfiture had been more or less inevitable from that moment.

To this extent the 1979 administration reflects an almost perfect contrast. To the horror of its critics and opponents, and the dismay of many of its supporters, it persisted with its basic strategy, notwithstanding a horrendous rise in unemployment and factory closures which had not remotely been foreseen; and in due course it was rewarded with a landslide parliamentary majority for a second term. What follows in these pages is not an attempt to prove that perseverance brought its own reward.

That would be a double oversimplification, both because the adherence to a single overriding strategy was often stricter in the rhetoric than the performance, but also because the 1983 landslide had many other causes. My purpose rather is to perform an inevitably very preliminary analysis of how and why the first Thatcher administration, though starting from a strikingly similar diagnosis of the ills of late twentieth-century Britain, followed a very different path; and to hazard some guesses about the extent to which it may, or may not, have brought about fundamental and lasting changes in the management of our affairs.

There has been a plethora of slim volumes about the 'Thatcher experiment' already, ranging from the almost-hagiographical to the downright feline. This is, however, so far as I am aware, the first contribution from a (late-coming and minor) participant, who had the privilege to see at least some of the action from inside. The standpoint is therefore inevitably different from that of my review of the Heath administration. Over the two years which intervened between the 1979 election and my recruitment to the Treasury I made no secret of my support for the basic approach of government, and I have not changed my mind in retrospect. But I was never an uncritical supporter: I believed that some serious mistakes were made, which complicated what would in any case have been a daunting task; and here too I have not changed my mind. The errors of a well-intentioned government can also teach us much about the governmental process.

As this account was being written the battle-lines between the 'radicals' and the 'consolidators' in the second Thatcher Government were already being drawn, and its record and performance will no doubt be influenced by the outcome of that argument (although its fate is far more likely to be decided by events in the wider world, and the performance and behaviour of the respective opposition parties). So predictions about the verdict of historians on the premiership of Mrs Thatcher would be as perilous as they would be premature.

I do not attempt them. My purpose instead is to survey the performance of a single Parliament, and one which happens – or so it seems to me – to have been unusually homogeneous. Certainly it was a Parliament dominated by one remarkable woman; but it is, I believe, quite erroneous to present the first Thatcher Government as a one-woman band. So my subject is a whole administration: the extent to which it did, and did not, break new ground, with some – highly provisional – apportionment of credit and of guilt for the achievements and the disappointments of four traumatic years.

Joseph de Maistre's dictum that 'every country has the Government it deserves' would be far too sweeping nowadays; but as far as our democracy goes there is, on balance, something in it. I believe we do deserve a second Thatcher Government, and I mean that to our credit. It is for the reader to decide whether I have made my case.

1 The Emergence of an Outsider

Mrs Margaret Thatcher is the first outsider to reach 10 Downing Street since Bonar Law. Several others – Ramsay MacDonald, Ted Heath, Jim Callaghan – may have started from the wrong side of the tracks. But long before they reached the pinnacle of the political system all of them had been welcomed to the Club. Not so Mrs Thatcher. She may have joined the Carlton Club as its first female member after election to the leadership of the Tory Party: but in the true sense she is not a joiner. No matter how long she remains at Downing Street, she will never be absorbed by the Establishment.

She was nobody's first choice to try to seize the baton from Edward Heath. Not even her own. In the aftermath of the second Labour victory in 1974 – indeed perhaps before – she had made her mind up that there had to be a change of leadership for her party. And she had her candidate for the task. He was Sir Keith Joseph.

Following the February 1974 election the two of them had secured the grudging consent of Edward Heath to the establishment of an out-house Think Tank called the Centre for Policy Studies, to research the elements of a 'Social Market Economy', to some extent in competition with the in-house Conservative Research Department. Basing himself at the CPS, where a tiny part-time staff (including the present author) was assembled, Sir Keith set about the delivery of a series of speeches during the summer of 1974 which attracted widespread coverage and which – to the fury of the party leader – amounted to a remarkably frank acknowledgement of errors perpetrated by the recent Tory Government.

Unfortunately the series culminated in a speech which included a somewhat naive and ill-judged passage (based upon

1

an article in the weekly *New Society*) which was open to the
interpretation that Sir Keith was attacking the feckless breed-
ing habits of the lower classes. That caused an uproar.
Characteristically, Sir Keith made matters worse by ignoring
the advice that Bernard Shaw gave to politicians: 'never
explain, never apologise'. Sir Keith explained and apologised
at length. Heads shook – Sir Keith's included. He rapidly
concluded that he was not the man to challenge Edward Heath,
and, again with characteristic self-effacement, urged Margaret
Thatcher to assume the task. Not without reluctance, she
agreed to do so.

Soon after the second Tory defeat in October 1974 it became
apparent that the backbenchers were of a mind to have a
contest for the leadership. It was a hazardous enterprise. The
grassroots swiftly rallied round Ted Heath. (The writer's own
constituency executive, which had clamoured for a change of
leadership on the morrow of the February 1974 defeat, now
called for continuity.) Many backbenchers, who wanted ultimately a change, felt the time was not ripe. The Shadow
Cabinet, with rare exceptions apart from Sir Keith and Mrs
Thatcher herself, was solidly behind the leader. And one
prophecy could be made with confidence: if Ted Heath
survived the challenge, the challengers could whistle for future
preferment.

Mrs Thatcher was undeterred. She was fortunate indeed to
enlist the services, as her campaign manager, of Airey Neave,
no mean student of the arts of black propaganda. His major
achievement was to secure a general underestimate of the scale
of votes pledged to his candidate. This induced complacency in
the Heath stable, and – vital in the current state of the Tory
backbenches – anxiety that he would run away with the contest
among many who had little inclination to vote for a woman
leader. The other prominent potential candidates held aloof,
out of loyalty or timidity: Hugh Fraser, a Rupert-of-the-Rhine
character who had occasionally thrown a disdainful gauntlet at
Mr Heath as Premier, but who had not held office since the
days of Alec Home, was the only other contender in the first
round of the contest. To almost everyone's amazement Mrs
Thatcher led the field. Mr Heath withdrew. Then those who

had hitherto kept their powder dry presented themselves: Willie Whitelaw, Jim Prior, Geoffrey Howe, John Peyton. But for all of them it was too late. Fortune favoured the brave. Mrs Thatcher came home in a canter.

Even then she had some way to go. By all accounts the vast majority of the Shadow Cabinet had voted for Ted Heath on the first round, and for candidates other than Mrs Thatcher on the second. She started as she was to continue: to an extent unique in the history of the modern Tory Party the standard-bearer of the rank and file, whom the elites viewed with bemusement, apprehension or downright antipathy.

She did not seek to impose her own stamp on the Shadow Cabinet. Peter Walker and Geoffrey Rippon, two senior members of the Heath administration, preferred to return to the backbenches; Robert Carr withdrew to the Lords and business; but against that Reggie Maudling, who had withdrawn from the Heath government (because of his previous business connections with John Poulson, an architect who had gone bankrupt amid allegations of corruption), but whose sympathies were more obviously with the former dispensation than the new, returned as Shadow Foreign Secretary – though not, as it turned out, for long: in due course he was to depart with a sulpherous resignation letter, although conflicts of opinion were sadly not the only reason then. John Biffen, a notably independent backbencher with a considerable House of Commons following, who had in the past been identified in sympathy with Enoch Powell, and who had responded to an invitation from Ted Heath to join his Shadow Cabinet in the summer of 1974 with the reservation that he should be free to continue to campaign for a change of leadership – a reservation that his leader had understandably rejected – also now joined the team. The changes, though, were modest, and left the new leader of the Opposition in a decided minority on her own front bench.

Reshaping the Shadow Cabinet was the first task for the new Opposition leader. She had next to establish her position in Parliament. This was not easy. Twice a week, on Tuesday and Thursday afternoons, Mrs Thatcher came out battling from her place opposite the despatch box at Prime Minister's

Question Time. Twice a week, as regular as clockwork, she bit the canvas. When, after fifteen months, Harold Wilson gave way to Jim Callaghan, things improved, but the contest remained unequal. Truth to tell there was nothing remotely surprising about this spectacle. Alec Douglas-Home, the only spiritual amateur among modern British Prime Ministers, had kept his end up against Harold Wilson the Leader of the Opposition, in the dying days of the 1959 Parliament. Ted Heath in Opposition rarely scored a point against Harold Wilson between 1965 and 1970; yet when the roles were reversed he rarely missed one. And in due course, when Mrs Thatcher herself acceded to the purple, her effortless superiority over Michael Foot, one of the great parliamentarians of his generation, was marvellous to behold. Prime Minister's questions are a hopelessly unequal contest in which the tenant of 10 Downing Street always has the last word and the leader of the Opposition might as well stay silent, but cannot afford to do so.

Her position was, however, even more insecure than the theatre of the House of Commons regularly made it seem. The Tory grandees looked upon her as little better than an aberration. They had tolerated Ted Heath rather as their forebears had tolerated Disraeli: not one of them, of course, but prepared to learn, and the best advocate for the cause who happened to be currently available. Mrs Thatcher was all too obviously not prepared to learn, and by no means self-evidently the best advocate available either. In the better class of political dining-room she rapidly became an object of derision, and the speculation turned around the identity of her successor when she had lost the next election. Members of her Shadow Cabinet indulged in analyses of her character as the port was circulating which occasionally induced the bystander to wonder why they agreed to serve under her leadership.

There was a reverse side to the coin. Many Tory backbenchers felt that, for the first time since the Second World War at least, they had a leader who instinctively reflected the priorities and the prejudices of the private members: and one who cultivated their constituency grassroots with sympathy whenever she was asked to do so. Churchill had been far too grand to concern himself with such trivia; Macmillan had viewed the benches behind him and the grassroots with a wary distaste; Douglas-Home had been willing and adored, but inexperienced; Heath had preferred the Whitehall village. Thatcher was the *conservatrice moyenne*, and her less eminent followers warmed to her. That would not have saved her from the adverse verdict of the Milk Street mafia (a title conferred upon the Executive of the 1922 Committee, the shop stewards of the Tory backbenches, when they met at the Milk Street office of their chairman, Edward du Cann, at the time of the 1975 Tory leadership election) had the verdict of the nation gone against her in 1979. Ted Heath had survived defeat in 1966 with ease; his successor's courtiers had no illusions about her ability to repeat his performance. But meanwhile her *rapport* with the rank and file ensured that they embarked upon the 1979 election campaign, when it came, with exceptional enthusiasm.

The fate of Oppositions and their leaders in the British parliamentary system is, however, rarely decided by their own performances. Whether Mrs Thatcher was to be the first female Prime Minister, or remembered as little more than a spasm in the backwoods before the Establishment resumed its reign, depended essentially on the record of the Labour government then in power.

Like every other government for twenty years, Labour had changed course – perhaps one should say turned turtle – halfway through its mandate. By the autumn of 1976 Chancellor Denis Healey's attempt to borrow his way out of the repercussions of the first 'oil shock' had run out of time and credibility. Not only were there no more lenders, but some of those who had left their cash in London – the Nigerian Government was a prominent example – had made up their minds to cut and run. Chancellor Healey suffered the ultimate humiliation of having the collapse of foreign confidence in sterling catch up with him just as he was boarding his plane at Heathrow on his way to play the international statesman at the annual meeting of the 'Fund and Bank'. He had to throw his briefs to his officials and catch a taxi straight back to Great George Street.

The medicine which the International Monetary Fund eventually induced the Labour Government, with great gnashing of teeth, to swallow, involving huge reductions in its public spending programmes and its deficit financing, coupled with a public commitment to the observance of target limitations to monetary growth, achieved a rapid restoration of the health of sterling, and, contrary to the vociferous forebodings of Labour's left wing and many independent commentators, did not lead to a disastrous rise in unemployment. On the contrary, unemployment fell.

Prior to these dramatic events the Labour Government had apparently improved its prospects in two respects. Harold Wilson had unexpectedly thrown in the towel, and Jim Callaghan had succeeded him. Whether Callaghan was a better Prime Minister than Mark II Wilson will be for the historians eventually to judge – there are some substantial items on the debit side of the ledger. But he was, by then, a more formidable performer in the House of Commons, on television and on the stump around the country: not an easy man to beat, with the authority of his office behind him. And to compensate for the loss – through by-election defeats – of the wafer-thin parliamentary majority that Wilson had secured in October 1974, Callaghan had fixed a remarkable deal with David Steel, the leader of the Liberals. Exploiting Steel's enthusiasm for partnerships (particularly with socialists), he secured Liberal support in return for nothing very tangible: although the Liberals had him at their mercy, since their opposition would have brought the Labour Government down at a time of maximum unpopularity, Steel extracted no commitment to his party's most essential objective, proportional representation. Joel Barnett, Labour's Chief Secretary to the Treasury, was later to complain that the Liberal economic spokesman, John Pardoe, was 'never out of my office'. But however great the inconvenience of this infliction – and it must have been considerable – it was a small price to pay for the time to restore the Labour Party's fortunes.

Judging by the evidence not only of opinion polls but also (more reliable between General Elections) of by-elections, however, the restoration was, to put it mildly, sluggish. By the autumn of 1978 Callaghan was coming up against the clock. He had at most twelve more months to play with; and when his union paymasters met for their annual conference in Brighton, his address to them was widely and no doubt correctly interpreted as a signal for an autumn election, even though, like many Prime Ministers before and since, he indulged in teasing the media on the subject. It therefore came as something of a bombshell when days later he appeared before the television cameras to tell the nation that he had decided to carry on through the winter after all.

There followed 'the winter of discontent'. The conventional wisdom has it that by scratching the contest in the autumn of 1978 Callaghan threw away his mandate: that had he gone to the country then he would probably have won; whereas by waiting he treated the country to the spectacle of unusually unpopular disruption of public services by his union allies, of which the sick, the old and the disabled were the best-publicised victims, in the ensuing winter, and thereby dished his chances.

There is of course no means of knowing whether Labour could have won a General Election in the autumn of 1978; and every reason to believe that the collision between government and unions in the public sector in the early months of 1979 alienated voters and undermined such credibility as attached to Labour's claim that it alone could manage the country's industrial relations. But the assumption that Callaghan blundered fatally by not calling the election before the onset of a difficult winter wage round is surely based on a misconception of Prime Ministerial priorities in the matter of election timing.

For the ruling party, at any given time, while to win must be the purpose, a narrow defeat is infinitely preferable to a more substantial rout a few months later. For some Cabinet Ministers, with their own future ambitions to think about, a narrow defeat may even be preferable to a victory which will confirm the existing Prime Minister in office. But for the Prime Minister – and for the Prime Minister alone – victory is all, since defeat is liable to lead to a clamour for a change of leadership. To the incumbent of Number 10 if defeat – even by a narrow margin – is on the cards it must always be preferable to put it off in the hope that something may turn up. Callaghan deferred the contest in the autumn of 1978 for one obvious reason: Labour's private opinion polls of the crucial West Midlands in September suggested that the government was likely to lose. That was quite sufficient grounds to run the risk of facing what the winter might bring forth.

Be that as it may, while the delay quite possibly ensured that Mrs Thatcher would go to Downing Street with a clear working majority for a Parliament which might earlier have been denied her, it also considerably enhanced the scale and variety of the hazards that would face her when she came to power. Throughout 1977 Chancellor Healey liked to look forward in private (and occasionally more or less in public) to what he called 'SOD': 'sod off day', or the day when the supervisors imposed by the IMF upon his handling of the UK economy following his appeal for help in the autumn of 1976 would pack their bags and leave him to his own devices.

It came earlier than expected. The collapse of overseas confidence in sterling before the IMF rescue had, as usual with market movements, been overdone; and when the Labour Government's deep retrenchment of public expenditure programmes had won the seal of IMF approval, together with a large loan, the turn-around was swift. By the autumn of 1977 the current account of the balance of payments, aided by a temporary plateau in world oil prices and the start of significant production from the North Sea, had moved into surplus, and with the dollar under a heavy cloud the smart money had begun to move into sterling on an increasing scale. For a time the Treasury and the Bank of England tried to hold the exchange rate down against it, slashing minimum lending rate from 14 per cent to 6 per cent in twelve months, accumulating reserves and starting to repay loans contracted over the three previous years ahead of time. But at the end of October 1978, the Bank of England, alarmed at the repercussions of this stand on domestic liquidity, had finally persuaded Chancellor Healey to let the exchange rate go. It bounced up 2½ points in a day. In December Healey wrote the IMF a second 'letter of intent' on the anniversary of his first, only this time saying in effect: 'look what a good boy am I.' The leading reins were off.

Healey lost no time in using his freedom. Although an intellectual apostle of the monetary restraint of inflation (he once told a City audience, with typical hyperbole, that no previous British Government since the war had given such precedent to monetary policy), by instinct he was a party politician first, last and all the time. With an election at most 18 months away the April 1978 Budget was his last chance to get the cash moving in pursuit of defecting Labour voters. Drawing attention to the movement of inflation into single figures for the first time since 1973, the fact that public expenditure pro- grammes for the year then ending, although slashed in November 1976, had been further underspent by some 4½ per cent, and the estimate that the money supply had only just exceeded his target (in fact it subsequently turned out to have overshot it by a wide margin, but no matter), he cut taxes by £2500m and increased spending programmes by £1000m. He admitted that his official soothsayers reckoned all this would raise the retail price index by 1 per cent in the summer of 1979. But against this he repeated a ritual formula which had come to feature in all his public pronouncements, and according to which there was a mechanical relationship between the level of wage settlements and the inflation outturn: a relationship which he was no doubt as well aware as any of his critics to be nonsensical, but which was intended to impress the gentlemen of the TUC. He set a monetary target of 8 to 12 per cent, a point below the (handsomely overshot) target for 1977–8, and hoped against experience for the best.

The best did not materialise. Unemployment continued to fall, but it had been falling for nine months already, and even the most dedicated neo-Keynesian would have been hard pressed to attribute the maintenance of the trend to the measures in the 1978 Budget. On the other hand, both inflation and interest rates soon began to rise as commodity prices – and particularly oil – began to reflect accelerating activity rates around the world. Minimum lending rate, raised to 7½ on Budget Day, moved steadily up to 10 per cent in June, 12½ per cent in November, and 14 per cent in February 1979. The retail price index, predicted to grow by an extra 1 per cent by June 1979, actually put on more than 2 per cent by March.

Against this background the attempt to impose another year's restraint on wages in the winter of 1978 was a pretty forlorn cause (although the feeling that Callaghan had led them up the garden path over the timing of the election undoubtedly diminished the readiness of the union bosses to make even a gesture on his behalf). The Cabinet plumped for 5 per cent. In retrospect – and when upbraided in the years ahead by union leaders who were anxious to spread responsibility for the electoral debacle which was shortly to engulf both partners – Denis Healey and other Labour ministers were prone to admit they had been too ambitious. It is hard to believe that any higher figure – short of the 12 per cent or thereabouts the more ambitious shop floors had their sights on – would have fared much better. Even if the union bosses' hearts had been in it, they had long ago forfeited the ability to deliver the cooperation of the membership. But the attempt to hold the line at 5 per cent in the public services guaranteed a turbulent winter.

Meanwhile the international environment was once more changing dramatically. Between mid-1977 and the end of 1978 the world price of oil had hardly moved. This meant that since oil is denominated in dollars, and the dollar was about as highly esteemed as the bubonic plague at that time, the 'real' price of oil was tumbling sharply. By the late autumn of 1978 the oil producers were becoming restive. Then the Shah fell, and shortly thereafter Persian oil exports dried up. A cold snap in the Northern hemisphere early in the New Year completed the transformation. Oil prices on the spot market took off, jumping $3 to $16.75 per barrel in January, and to $23.15 by February. By May some deals were being done at $40 per barrel.

One further bear-trap was laid in the spring of 1979; and with that, the obstacle course prepared by Labour and the gods for the next government would be complete. Shortly after Christmas Callaghan travelled out to the West Indies for a summit meeting. There were press reports about the world leaders relaxing under the palm trees, and the British Prime Minister returned to a country in the grip of winter and industrial strife. The newspapers were full of graphic details of hospitals under seige, and homes for the sick and disabled denied essential supplies. Descending from his plane at Heathrow, Callaghan was greeted by waiting journalists who were far more interested in his reactions to events at home than in his reminiscences of statesmanship on the other side of the Atlantic. How did he propose to tackle the crisis, he was asked. 'Crisis?', he replied, 'What crisis?'

It was one of those asides, like Harold Macmillan's comment

about the country never having had it so good, and Harold Wilson's assurance that the 1967 devaluation did not apply to 'the pound in your pocket', which promptly entered the national consciousness, with effects that had never been foreseen by their authors. The impression was created, however unfairly, of a Prime Minister dangerously out of touch with the harsh realities of life in the streets. Labour's lowly standing in the opinion polls sank still further.

The government faced an uncomfortable dilemma. Continuation of the disruption in the public services was increasingly unpopular. Resentment might be focused on the unions which were orchestrating the trouble; but much of it rubbed off on the Labour Government, which could not easily distance itself from the unions when the main plank of its platform for the next election was to be its unique ability to get along with them. Yet to buy a return to work with settlements substantially in excess of the chosen limit of 5 per cent would constitute an equally damaging humiliation.

Callaghan found a characteristic escape route. He announced the establishment of a 'Comparability Commission' under the chairmanship of Professor Clegg from Warwick University, one of the doyens of the industrial arbitration industry and a one-time member of Harold Wilson's Prices and Incomes Board. This body was to be given the task of investigating relative rates of pay in the public and private sectors, and recommending appropriate wage adjustments, where needed to restore 'comparability', in the former. The government undertook in advance to honour such recommendations. On that basis the public sector unions agreed to return to 'normal working'. So the 'winter of discontent' was concluded with open-ended and postdated cheques: cheques which it would fall to the next government to honour.

All that remained to be settled was the timing of the General Election. The general impression was that Callaghan was now reckoning on a late summer contest to allow time for memories of the winter's conflicts to fade, and for living standards to accumulate a little more fat. But at the beginning of March a fresh encumbrance was thrown across his path. A vast amount of the time during the October 1974 Parliament had been taken up with Bills for the establishment of devolved Assemblies in

Scotland and Wales. Most English MPs responded to these measures with a massive yawn. But the Labour Government needed them to placate the nationalist MPs from the two countries, whose support, or at least abstention, was essential for its survival once its parliamentary majority had gone. Unfortunately one or two of the most skilful and determined parliamentarians on the government backbenches were implacably opposed to devolution: and in alliance with the Tories they had attached amendments to the Bills by which referenda were to be held in Scotland and in Wales before they would take effect. These referenda were held at the beginning of March. That in Wales produced a crushing majority against devolution; while that in Scotland produced a narrow favourable majority, but far less than the two-thirds vote demanded by the amendments. The government reacted by reaffirming its intention to proceed with the Scottish Bill. But plainly there was now no chance of progress before the General Election. The Scottish Nationalists reckoned they had been betrayed: they wanted blood.

The Shadow Cabinet agonised about the way to exploit the situation. The government could still count on the support of the two Scottish Labour MPs who had left the party over devolution, and possibly the three Welsh Nationalists and one or both of the two anti-Unionist MPs from Northern Ireland. Even if all the Liberals, Ulster Unionists and Scottish Nationalists voted with the Tories – and that too was uncertain, particularly in view of the fact that many of the Nationalists were likely to lose their seats in an early General Election – the outcome of a vote of no confidence would still be too close to call. Yet if a motion of no confidence were to fail it could not, by parliamentary convention, be repeated for many weeks. In the end, however, Mrs Thatcher, taking her courage in both hands, made up her mind to go ahead.

The result was the most electric night the House of Commons had experienced within the service of any of its Members. As the afternoon wore on it was known that one Labour backbencher was too ill to attend. Against that it was reported that both the anti-Unionists from Ulster intended to support the government; while one of the Unionists announced his intention to do the same. By the time the vote was called at

10 p.m. no one seemed to know with confidence what the outcome would be: a government majority of one or two; an Opposition majority of one or two; or perhaps a tie, with the Speaker giving his casting vote, according to the rules, in favour of the government.

While the votes were being counted the present author approached the Speaker to thank him for calling him to speak during the course of the debate. 'It looks', I said, 'as though you're going to have to use your casting vote.' 'I don't think so', was the reply, 'I think the government will be home by one.' But when the tellers marched in to report the outcome it was immediately apparent that both of us were wrong. The government had indeed been defeated, by one vote. Callaghan promised an immediate dissolution.

*   *   *

Legend has it that the Tory Party won the May 1979 election by pinning on the Labour Government responsibility for creating mass unemployment. The message was encapsulated in the advertisement devised by the Tories' new advertising agents, Saatchi & Saatchi, depicting a long, winding dole queue with the slogan 'Labour isn't working'. But in fact the celebrated Saatchi advertisement did not date from the 1979 election at all. It appeared on the hoardings in the early autumn of 1978. That does not mean that its place in Labour's demonology is undeserved. On the contrary. For the Saatchi campaign of September 1978 is one of the rare instances where political advertising almost certainly produced a tangible result. Not the Tory victory of May 1979. But the decision of the then Prime Minister not to risk an appeal to the country seven months earlier. It was after these advertisements appeared to have achieved a shift in public sentiment against the government that Callaghan took his soundings in the West Midlands, and got the dusty answer which persuaded him to put off the evil day.

Unemployment was not, however, a major issue in the election when eventually it came. While there were still more than one and a quarter million people out of work, the last monthly statistics published before the nation polled produced the biggest fall in numbers in a single month for more than 15 years; and while Tory spokesmen repeated the reminder that every Labour Government left the dole queues longer than it found them, whereas every Tory Government since the war had left them shorter, the fact that unemployment had more than doubled since Labour had taken over in February 1974 inhibited ministers, and the fact that it was currently falling steeply inhibited attacks by the Opposition. In any case it was far from foremost among the priorities of the general public.

Coping with the unions; taxation; law and order; beating inflation: these were the main themes of the month-long campaign. On all of them the Tories had the edge. Labour's boast that it alone could harness union cooperation had blown back in its face, although the warning that a Tory Government would lead to 'head-on confrontation' still had some power to frighten voters who recalled the dénouement of the Heath administration. Against this, the yearning for some restraint on union militancy had been vastly reinforced by the events of the early spring, and Tory promises of legislation to curb abuses struck a strong response. The hyperinflation of the middle-1970s had dragged millions across the tax threshold, and hugely increased the numbers paying higher rates of income tax. So the Tory promise to reduce direct taxation, and to shift some of the burden of 'fructifying the revenue' to indirect taxes, was calculated to be popular with large sections of the electorate for whom in any previous election taxation would have been at best of marginal concern.

Law and order, with all that that implied, were also – not unusually – on the Tories' side. Labour was widely held to be soft on criminality, and therefore to blame for the inexorable advance of the tide of crimes of violence. In truth the Tory campaign was rather longer on denunciation than on specific proposals to reverse the tide. The police force, whose morale had been sapped by Labour's propensity to make it toe the line of wage control, would be brought back up to strength, and there would be a new regime of 'short, sharp shocks' for young offenders. But the Tories plainly had not the least intention of acceding to the aspiration foremost in the minds of 'law and order' voters, by bringing back the noose and/or birch. Never mind: the noises sounded right, whereas Labour's didn't.

On each of these issues – unions, taxation and law and order

– the debate was essentially about means, not ends. Labour did not dissent from propositions that the unions must improve their ways; that taxation was excessive; and that 'something should be done' about crime: its claim was rather that it was now the 'party of government' and experience which knew how to go about it. On the control of inflation there was a sharper cleavage between the parties. Labour boasted (or at least Chancellor Healey did) of its record of monetary orthodoxy and its introduction of the concept of cash controls in public spending: but the kernel of its counter-inflation policy was its reasserted understanding with the unions. The Tory Party spoke with more than one voice on wage control: Jim Prior was inclined to endorse Labour's 'tripartite approach' (i.e. based on negotiation with the TUC and CBI), whereas Mrs Thatcher made no secret of her impatience with such corporatist devices. But there was no disposition in the Opposition ranks to revive the pledge inserted in the 1970 campaign to cut price rises in the public sector 'at a stroke'. Instead the emphasis was laid upon the monetary control of inflation at source, assisted by the encouragement of competition. There is, however, no evidence that this argument swayed a lot of votes on either side.

If the Tories had in general the more appealing slogans, though, Labour had one substantial asset: the personality of its leader. Mrs Thatcher was by no means the first Opposition leader to trail her party's ratings in the opinion polls by a wide margin: Ted Heath had suffered a similar experience from 1966–70, and had yet gone on to win. But Jim Callaghan was universally acknowledged to be a formidable performer, who transmitted an impression of calm authority and common sense every time he came before the television cameras. Mrs Thatcher, by contrast, often sounded strident and abrasive. Notwithstanding the traumas of the spring, Jim Callaghan looked the choice of safety, Mrs Thatcher the choice of hazard. Had Britain had a presidential system, there is not much doubt who would have won on 3 May: throughout the campaign, voters asked by the pollsters to nominate their preference for premier gave Callaghan a comfortable lead. But since the contest in Britain is between parties, there was in truth but little doubt which of the two would emerge the victor. Labour narrowed the gap, certainly – and in one aberrant poll at the beginning of the final week of the campaign actually took the lead – while the Liberals gained ground markedly. But with that one exception, all the polls predicted that Mrs Thatcher would have an overall majority. As soon as the first results were flashed onto the television screens shortly before midnight on 3 May, it was confirmed that Britain was to have the first woman Prime Minister in its history, backed by the largest swing between the major parties since 1945.

2 A Cabinet of Conflict

Eight years ago the present author and the present Chancellor of the Exchequer published an analysis of decision-making in government (*The Power Game*, Macmillan, 1976). One of the generalisations hazarded in the conclusions was that Prime Ministers with an election triumph under their belts start with enormous authority, but that 'it wears with use, and still more with abuse'. In this, as in so many other respects, Mrs Thatcher was an exception to the rule.

As already recorded, she had not attempted to create a Shadow Cabinet remotely in her own image when she captured the leadership of the party in 1975. That was probably wise. Her own ministerial experience had been unusually limited for a party leader; she knew that the large majority of her front bench colleagues had not favoured her candidacy; she had to extend and secure her base. But after 3 May 1979 things were different. She had led the party back from the wilderness it dislikes so much. The world was her oyster. Had she chosen to form a government of likeminded men and women, there were none to say her nay.

Prior to the election the impression had been created that that indeed would be her intention. In a series of press interviews over the years in Opposition the impression had been given that she would have little time for argument in Cabinet – less, perhaps, even than her predecessor, who had not been noted for his patience with dissent. Yet when it came to the point she formed a Cabinet where there were, at best, nine voices to be counted on, and at least a similar number of potential rebels, several of whom had made no secret of their distaste for both her opinions and her style in Opposition. Outside the Cabinet her supporters were rather more strongly represented. There, too, however, there were plenty of known critics in the lower ranks of the administration.

According to Whitehall legend, she had effectively put the composition of her government into commission. Most incoming Prime Ministers take soundings of their senior colleagues at such moments. Harold Macmillan once described how, following the Tory victory of 1951, Churchill took him off to lunch at Boodle's to discuss the allocation of positions, and his embarrassment on discovering that neither he nor his host happened to be members of that celebrated St James's watering-place (fortunately no one, it seems, challenged their presence). But by all accounts the scale of devolution in June 1979, to Willie Whitelaw, the faithful lieutenant, to Humphrey Atkins, the outgoing Chief Whip, and to Michael Jopling, Atkins's chosen successor, was unusual.

Since no British Prime Minister, contrary to some recent constitutionalists, is ever more than *primus inter pares*, conformity can be overdone. It is at least arguable that Ted Heath would have stood a better chance of survival after his double defeat in 1974 had his Cabinet been a broader church. But the distribution of portfolios in 1979 was taken to surprising lengths of catholicism. The Treasury, with Sir Geoffrey Howe as Chancellor, John Biffen as Chief Secretary, Nigel Lawson as Financial Secretary, and Peter Rees and Lord Cockfield as Ministers of State, was seen as 'sound' (from a Thatcherite point of view): although John Biffen, an unrepentant monetarist, was far too much a sceptic and a pessimist in the Whig tradition to succumb to enthusiasm for this or any other school of economics.

The other major economic departments were given somewhat less coherent teams. At Industry Sir Keith Joseph, it was said, when asked whom he would like to have to support him, replied that he would be delighted with any suitable appointments. In Adam Butler, son of RAB, he received a Minister for Industry, with responsibility for the public sector, who did not obviously share his abstemious approach. At Trade, John Nott was joined by two Ministers of State, Sally Oppenheim and Cecil Parkinson, who shared commitment to the open market and the motif of competition. But at Employment Jim Prior had a team which was solidly identified with his own unrepentant corporatism.

Elsewhere the Foreign Office, with Lord Carrington in charge and Ian Gilmour, also in the Cabinet, as the principal spokesman in the Commons, had but one Minister, Nicholas Ridley, who was reckoned to share the Prime Minister's philosophy, and the Foreign Secretary was careful to appoint him to the Latin American periphery. At Education Mark Carlisle, the Secretary of State, was not particularly identified with a specific stratum of the party spectrum; but it was widely noted that Dr Rhodes Boyson, an articulate proponent of the social market who had often struck a divergent note from Mark Carlisle when they had together shadowed Education in the years of Opposition, had been consigned to the lowly rank of Parliamentary Under-Secretary, with the more reassuring personality – reassuring, that is, to the establishment of the state education system – of Lady Young promoted above him as Minister of State. Michael Heseltine, the florid and ambitious darling of the Tory Party Conference, was given the Prime Minister's former Parliamentary Private Secretary, John Stanley, as Minister of State to keep an eye on him at the Department of Environment, and another Minister of State, Tom King, who had for no very obvious reason missed out in the distribution of the prizes, having been a member of the Shadow Cabinet in Opposition. At Health and Social Security Patrick Jenkin, the Secretary of State, was an economiser by reputation, albeit one who had shown no obvious qualms in service during the faster-spending period of the previous Tory administration. His Ministers of State, former Labour turncoat Reg Prentice and Dr Gerry Vaughan, could be relied upon to keep their noses clean; but the Parliamentary Under-Secretaries, Sir George Young and Lynda Chalker, looked set to absorb the ethos of the Elephant and Castle as to the manor born. Willie Whitelaw came to the Home Office burdened with the expectations of the Tory law and order and immigration lobbies which he was certain to disappoint, and kitted out with subordinate ministers who were unlikely to cause the officials of his department a moment's unease. David Howell was rewarded for his services as speech and campaign coordinator before and during the election with elevation to the Cabinet as Secretary for Energy, a department where his own theoretical commitment to market forces would be balanced by the Scottish paternalism of his Minister of State, Hamish Gray. Francis Pym, who had been Shadow Foreign Affairs spokesman in Opposition, was required not unreluctantly to yield pride of place to Lord Carrington, apparently because his Lordship was not minded to serve elsewhere, and consoled with the Ministry of Defence. A trimmer by nature, he moved to Defence with perhaps some sense of resentment, and backed up by his formidable Permanent Secretary, Sir Frank Cooper, was soon to emerge as a champion of expenditure. To Northern Ireland went Humphrey Atkins, who had worked closely with the Prime Minister as Chief Whip in Opposition, and who was not expected to beat the province's formidable reputation as the graveyard of ministerial ambition. For Wales and Scotland Nicholas Edwards and George Younger respectively chose themselves (in Younger's case because the Shadow Scottish spokesman, Teddy Taylor, had suffered an *accident de parcours* in the General Election, losing his Glasgow seat to the immense relief of the Scottish civil service). At Agriculture, with Peter Walker as Minister and Alick Buchanan-Smith as Minister of State, the spirit of the Heath administration was resuscitated out of time, like Lord Palmerston as the last relic of the Regency surviving into the high Victorian era. And the administration was rounded off with two grandees, Lords Hailsham and Soames, to run the judiciary and Rhodesia respectively, who had one characteristic in common, that each believed he was more obviously endowed for 10 Downing Street than the new incumbent, and only denied his opportunity by a cruel quirk of fate; and a court jester, Norman St John-Stevas, as Leader of the House of Commons who, like the court jesters of old, was to prove himself endowed with a tongue which was too sharp for others' comfort, and ultimately his own. In sum, most departments received the ministers they would have chosen for themselves. It was a recipe for contention with a Prime Minister who was not herself by nature predisposed to sympathy with the ambitions of the civil service.

There was, however, one notable omission. Mrs Thatcher had to contend with one problem unknown to any other modern Prime Minister on assuming office: what to do with the predecessor whom she had unseated. It was, of course, by no means unprecedented for a former Prime Minister to be available for further service under his successor. Churchill had to accommodate Neville Chamberlain in 1940, and Heath Lord Home in 1970. But Churchill had formed a coalition government, and Chamberlain was in no position to resist him: besides, he was mortally sick. As for Lord Home, he had found little evident satisfaction in the role of Leader of the Opposition following the Tory defeat in October 1964, and had not needed much persuasion to surrender it in the following summer. He had then been happy to serve under his chosen successor as Foreign Secretary.

Ted Heath, by contrast, had been bitterly resentful of the manner of his eviction following the defeat of October 1974. He believed, with some justification, that the vote of the parliamentary Tory Party against him had not reflected the opinions of the party in the country; and also – again with justification – that that vote had represented a direct repudiation of his own administration. In the supervening years of Opposition the wounds had not healed: indeed they had festered. Heath complained in private, and on occasion in public as well, that his successor and her supporters had been 'rewriting history', and implying that the 1970 administration had been an aberration. Contacts between himself and Mrs Thatcher had been almost non-existent, and glacial when they had occurred.

Yet he retained a significant following on the Tory backbenches, and in the country; while overseas he was far better known than his successor, and widely recognised as a statesman of international status. Pious hopes had often been expressed that when the Tory Party returned to power its new leader and her predecessor would be reconciled, and that a suitable role would be found for him to fill.

This was a great deal easier said than done. When Heath had been Premier, and Mrs Thatcher Minister of Education, their relations in Cabinet had not been notably cordial. It was well nigh impossible to imagine them working comfortably in harness with the roles reversed. Besides, there were only two posts which anyone could imagine Heath accepting: the Treasury and the Foreign Office. Since economic policy was the area where the two were most obviously at loggerheads, to have made him Chancellor was unthinkable for the new Prime

Minister. As to the Foreign Office, it was bespoke for Lord Carrington. In any case, Heath's very experience and standing on the world stage would have meant that Mrs Thatcher would have felt herself overshadowed by her Foreign Secretary. Nor did they see eye to eye on a range of international issues, from aid to Europe.

Predictably, perhaps, the outcome of this dilemma only widened the yawning gulf between the two. Ten days after her victory the Prime Minister wrote to Heath to offer him the Washington Embassy. He replied curtly that 'as I have said, I do wish to stay in the Commons. I am sure you will be able to find somebody to do the job well.' He was reported to have found the offer mischievous in view of his well-attested preference for the backbenches if the Foreign Office were not available. She was reported to have found the leakage of their correspondence to the press mischievous. Both retired hurt.

In the event it is doubtful whether the absence of a reconciliation, and the presence of a baleful predecessor on her backbenches, did the new Prime Minister any harm in the years ahead. Indeed it may well on balance have strengthened her position when it was most vulnerable. Over almost the whole range of policy, and particularly over economic management and international relations, Heath became a persistent, outspoken and articulate critic (indeed his contributions to parliamentary debate from his chosen place 'below the gangway' – i.e. about eight feet along from Mrs Thatcher – were marked by an eloquence and wit which had seldom been in evidence when he had held her office). But both his persistence and his outspokenness were widely interpreted as motivated by personal resentment, and therefore found offensive in a party which has always combined ruthlessness towards an unsuccessful leader with absolute loyalty to him or her until the moment of failure comes. Other critics – both inside and outside the government itself – were to find their coded style inhibited by association. Sometimes incipient revolts were to be abandoned in the face of general party indignation at a Heathian broadside.

*   *   *

As soon as the Prime Minister and her Cabinet-makers had

picked the ministerial team they had to turn their attention to the economy.

The 1979 spring Budget had been a casualty of the Callaghan Government's defeat in the vote of confidence. Thereafter it had been agreed that Denis Healey should introduce a standstill Budget simply to secure parliamentary renewal for taxes that would otherwise have lapsed, leaving it to the victors in the imminent election to introduce a summer Budget and Finance Bill tailored to their priorities and intentions. This was now the urgent task of Sir Geoffrey Howe and his Treasury Ministers.

The background was not auspicious (in fairness, it very seldom is for incoming governments: the last months of a Parliament are never those for grasping nettles with the need to woo the voters uppermost in the minds of ministers). Output in 1978 was reckoned to have grown by some 3 per cent after several years of stagnation; but most of this growth had occurred in mid-year. By the autumn output was falling again, and the provisional figures for the spring of 1979 suggested a further fall, although these had been distorted by the industrial disputes in public services. Unemployment had been falling sharply, and by May 1979 was down to 1.3 million. The money supply, calculated by the chosen aggregate of £M3, had come out at $11\frac{1}{2}$ per cent, just within Chancellor Healey's target of 8 to 12 per cent. That was about the sum total of the good news, and none of it looked to be sustainable: monetary growth in particular was accelerating, and had been distorted by the imposition of the 'corset' of quantitative controls on bank deposits imposed by the Bank of England in the previous summer (although the full extent of this distortion was not guessed at until the garment was removed in 1980).

The bad news was that inflation, having fallen briefly to a six-year low of $7\frac{1}{2}$ per cent in the summer of 1978, was now once more over 10 per cent and on a rising trend. Public expenditure was reckoned to have grown by 6 per cent in the year just ended, after two years of severe contraction. The current account of the balance of payments had accumulated a £1000m deficit in the first four months of 1979; and while imports had grown by about 6 per cent between the first half of 1978 and the corresponding period of the following year (and imports of finished goods by more than twice as much), exports had fallen slightly. Worst of all, unit labour costs in manufacturing had risen by 12 per cent in 1978 – six times the rate in Germany – and were still accelerating, while sterling's effective exchange rate had risen by 5 per cent in a month in April, and the dollar rate was hovering over $2. When the real rate of return in manufacturing industry had dropped to little more than 2 per cent, the implications for employment and private sector solvency were ominous indeed.

On top of all of this there was Professor Clegg to reckon with. When Mr Callaghan had recalled this survivor from the heyday of incomes regulation in the 1960s to extricate his government from the 'winter of discontent' there had been fierce argument within the Tory Party in Opposition about how to respond. Those, led by Jim Prior, holding the Shadow Employment portfolio, who burned a candle for the corporate management of the economy in conjunction with the CBI and TUC, had argued from conviction that some formula of 'comparability' was going to be needed to achieve the peaceful resolution of wage claims in the public sector under a Tory Government, and therefore that it would be wise to treat the professor as a gift horse. Others argued that if the party was serious about its commitment to apply market disciplines to wage bargaining in the private sector, and to extend them as far as possible to the public sector too, it was vital that Clegg should be repudiated in advance. For the extension of market disciplines to the public sector implied that the level of wage settlements would – and must – have repercussions on the levels of service and employment which the public sector offered; whereas if government were committed in advance to honour whatever rise in salaries the Professor calculated to be justified by the logic of his remit, it could not very well refuse to find the extra cash to foot the bills without adjustment of either services or payrolls. (Joel Barnett, Chief Secretary to the Treasury in the Labour Government, had tried to argue in the House of Commons and outside that his colleagues' pledge to honour Clegg's awards, whatever they might be, was subordinate to the cash limits on individual blocks of public spending: his Prime Minister, with more logic if with characteristic irresponsibility, made it clear that that was not the policy of his government.) It was also argued from the Tory backbenches in Opposition that however strenuously an incoming Tory Government asserted its determination to leave the private sector to face the consequences of the way it fixed its wages, fashions are slow to die, and it would take time for private businesses to be weaned from the notion that what they paid was determined by what others – including public corporations and services – agreed to pay; and that consequentially exaggerated settlements that were bound to come from Clegg would have disastrous effects on costs, competitiveness and ultimately employment in the private sector. Keeping up with Clegg, it was said, would be far more lethal than keeping up with the Joneses.

In the end, though, the official response of the Tory Opposition to the establishment of the Clegg Commission was settled on more pragmatic grounds. There were more than 5 million people, most of them electors, who looked to the public sector for their weekly household incomes. Directly or indirectly they had expectations of short-term financial benefit from Clegg. The eve of an election was no time, it was decided, to offer them the frustration of their hopes. So the Shadow Cabinet publicly promised to honour the Labour Government's commitment to pay whatever Professor Clegg and Co advised it should. It is not only governments which refrain from grasping nettles on the eve of the electoral battles.

Nor was the public commitment to the Clegg reviews the only hostage given to fortune before and during the 1979 election. The scope for economy in public expenditure had also been severely circumscribed. Pledges had been given to preserve the purchasing power of long-term welfare benefits; to maintain – at least – the real value of resources committed to the Health Service; to increase spending on defence by 3 per cent a year 'in real terms'; to restore forthwith the comparative value of police pay which the Labour Government had eroded; and thereafter to preserve the concept of 'comparability' for policemen and members of the armed forces, whatever might happen elsewhere. There had even been somewhat unguarded rejections by Mrs Thatcher of Labour campaign claims that the Tories planned to raise prescription charges and double the rate of VAT; while letters had been despatched in response to enquiries from members of the public about the Tories' intentions towards the payment of public sector employees such as the firemen (who had extracted pledges of future preferment from the Labour Government) which were to prove sources of embarrassment in the months ahead.

Labour's farewell plans for public spending, published in January 1979, had projected an increase of 2 per cent a year in total programmes at constant prices over the four years up to April 1983. Denis Healey had calculated that such a rate of spending would be consistent with a steady, if modest, contraction in the sums that government would need to borrow (the Public Sector Borrowing Requirement) from £7300m in 1978/9 to £6800m in 1981/2, and with taxes and tax allowances simply revalorised to allow for the impact of inflation. But this comforting prospect was based on a number of assumptions which looked highly optimistic when first published, and which in many cases had already been overtaken by events before his successor was installed in Great George Street. It was assumed that the economy would grow by $2\frac{3}{4}$ per cent a year on average – almost seven times the actual rate of growth over the four preceding years; that UK labour costs in manufacturing would rise by less than those of our competitors; that costs incurred by the public sector (the 'relative price effect') would grow more slowly still; and that the cost of servicing the government debt, after rising very modestly in 1979 and 1980, would stabilise and then fall. In the short term it was also assumed that earnings would rise by 7 per cent in 1979, for the simple reason that that was the figure calculated to be consistent with the government's 5 per cent pay ceiling. Sir Geoffrey Howe might have been forgiven if he had commented, like the Duke of Wellington, 'if you can believe that, you can believe anything'.

Yet the incoming Tory Government was committed by its manifesto to immediate reductions in direct taxation. Now there was a school of thought which had made great strides in fashionability in the later 1970s on the other side of the Atlantic, according to which tax cuts would generate so much additional activity that there was no need for accommodating cuts in public spending, since revenues would soar. The *locus classicus* for this tempting prescription, popularly christened 'supply side economics', was the state of California, where the electors had been persuaded to write into their ballot papers endorsement – binding upon the state government – of sweeping cuts in local taxes. It was held that these tax reductions had indeed stimulated the Californian economy, and thus enriched state revenues. What tended to be over-looked by the evangelists of 'Proposition 13' – the proposal that the voters had endorsed – was that the Californian state government had happened coincidentally to enjoy a massive budget surplus to cushion the shock of revenues foregone until the 'supply side' benefits materialised: which was not the fortunate position of the British or any other major national government in 1979.

The Republicans, led by the former Governor of California Ronald Reagan, were to sweep to power 18 months after Mrs Thatcher on a platform of 'supply side economics'. The British Tory Government elected in 1979, however, made no such comforting assumptions. On the contrary it had argued in Opposition that the level of public borrowing it was inheriting in May 1979 would need to be reduced substantially over time if the revival of the fortunes of private enterprise was not to be choked off by the level of interest rates required to fund the public debt without excessive monetary expansion. So if taxes upon income and borrowing were both to be reduced, where were the savings going to come from?

The present author had ventured to offer a number of specific suggestions, including the abandonment of the Labour Government's commitment (not in practice always honoured) to raise welfare benefits and pensions by as much as average earnings when that turned out to be higher than the rise in prices, reductions in the level of grants paid out as inducements to new manufacturing investment in areas of high unemploy-ment, and an obligation to be placed upon those in public sector employment who would become entitled to inflation-guaranteed pensions on retirement to meet the true actuarial cost of this privilege from their contributions. These sugges-tions were contained in an article published in the *Daily Telegraph* between the defeat of the Callaghan Government in the parliamentary vote of no confidence, and the launching of the ensuing General Election. They were not well received. In the event most of them were later enacted by the victorious

Tory Government. But at the time the *Daily Mirror* thought them worthy of front-page treatment under the headline 'the Knut from Knutsford' (the constituency for which the author had recently been returned in a by-election); Labour MPs printed them on broadsheets and professed to foresee that they would tilt the balance in the polling booths, and many Tory MPs feared likewise. The chairman of the Tory Party gently expressed the hope there would not be a sequel.

The party manifesto, at any rate, had been a lot more circumspect.

> Important savings can be made in several ways. We will scrap expensive Socialist programmes, such as the national-isation of building land. We shall reduce government intervention in industry and particularly that of the National Enterprise Board, whose borrowing powers are planned to reach £4.5bn. We shall ensure that selective assistance to industry is not wasted, as it was in the case of Labour's assistance to certain oil platform yards . . . The reduction of waste, bureaucracy, and over-government will also yield substantial savings. For example, we shall look for economies in the cost . . . of running our tax and social security systems. By comparison with private industry, local direct labour schemes waste an estimated £400m a year. Other examples of waste abound, such as the plan to spend £50m to build another town hall in Southwark.

It was a little reminiscent of the housewife who announces that she has salvaged the family budget by deciding not to buy a mink coat in the sales after all.

Specific economies, by contrast, were hard to find. 'There is', it was stated, 'a strong case for relating government assistance to [industrial] projects more closely to the number of jobs they create.' Shares in the National Freight Corporation would be offered to the public. And there was the prospect of additional revenue from two sources: 'we must . . . be prepared to switch to some extent from taxes on earnings to taxes on spending'; and 'restoring the will to work . . . involves bringing unem-ployment and short-term sickness benefit within the tax system'. That was about it: not much straw for Sir Geoffrey and his men to make their bricks from.

Nevertheless the Budget they came forward with just five weeks after the election victory marked a major change of course by any standards. The basic rate of tax was cut by 3 per cent from 33 to 30. Personal allowances were raised by 18 per cent – more than double the increase required to match the rise in prices since the previous Budget. The top marginal rate of tax on income from employment was slashed from 85 per cent to 60 per cent; and the top rate of tax on income from investments from Denis Healey's confiscatory 98 per cent to 75 per cent, while the starting-point for the tax was raised from £1700 in dividends to £5000. All this was calculated to cut the revenues from income tax by £3500m in the year to April 1980, which was to be recouped in part from a jump in the standard rate of VAT from 8 per cent to 15 (and a consolidation of the higher rate at that level), together with the traditional revalorisation of excise duties to take account of inflation. Even so, the Budget changes were expected to produce a net cut of £1000m in revenues.

On the other side of the ledger Sir Geoffrey revealed plans to slice £3500m out of public spending. Of this £1000m was to come from manpower economies induced by denying to departments all the extra cash needed to meet current and prospective public sector wage rises; £1500m from specific cuts in individual programmes; and £1000m from the sale of (unspecified) state assets. The result, it was estimated, would be to reduce government borrowing from a figure approaching £11 000m, which would otherwise have been in prospect, to about £8200m, or £1000m less than the actual amount that Labour had to borrow in its last year of office. To round off the picture, the target rate of growth for sterling M3 was set at 7–11 per cent, 1 per cent lower than that for 1978/9, and the Bank of England's minimum lending rate was raised by 2 per cent to 14 per cent.

The keynote of this first Budget was thus a very sharp shift from tax on earning to tax on spending. It was reckoned to add almost 4 per cent to the cost of living. But the hope was that employees, rewarded with a handsome increase in their take-home pay, would take this on the chin and not seek to recoup the cost of larger household bills from higher wages. To assist the process the Financial Secretary to the Treasury, Nigel Lawson, unveiled a brand new yardstick, the 'Tax and Prices Index', to supplement the traditional retail prices index with evidence of the value of income tax changes. It cannot be said that the new index ever took the public fancy (which was perhaps as well when it proved more difficult to repeat the June 1979 tax cuts in later years).

The intention of the Budget strategy, which had been clearly signalled during the election campaign, was to restore incentives which, it was reckoned, had been dangerously eroded by Labour's reliance on direct taxation. That this corresponded with popular priorities could hardly be gainsaid by any who had fought the 1979 election. Income tax, which not so very long ago had been a grievance of the *rentier* classes, had become a national bugbear. Labour politicians, leaders of the public service unions (but conspicuously not those who claimed to speak for those employed in private manufacturing) and neo-Keynesian economists naturally forecast that workers and their families would resent the compression of what they called the 'social wage' – welfare services and payments – and pooh-poohed the claim that lower taxes on their earnings would encourage the 'wealth creators' to work harder. They seized with particular delight upon a characteristically frank acknowledgement from Chief Secretary John Biffen. Challenged by a radio interviewer with the proposition that executives whose top marginal rate of taxation had been cut from 85 to 60 per cent might simply decide they could afford to spend more time on the golf course, John Biffen cheerfully agreed they might. What the critics could not easily refute, however, was that rates of tax of 85 and 98 per cent had more to do with the politics of envy than with raising revenue, and that the tax threshold had fallen exceptionally low by international standards as Labour had allowed the hyperinflation of the middle 1970s to sweep more millions into tax.

But while his first Budget responded to a popular perception, Sir Geoffrey did not stoop to gild the lily. On the contrary: his forecast was that following the Budget changes inflation would rise to 16 per cent by the year-end, thereafter dropping back to some 13½ per cent by mid-1980; and that output and living standards would fall. Although Chancellors wisely refrain from making predictions about unemployment it was obvious that a sharp reversal of the falling trend of recent months was expected.

The first and most important date for Tory Chancellors following completion of the Budget speech is a meeting later the same evening with the party's backbench Finance Committee. Sir Geoffrey was greeted with a full house and a rapturous reception. His colleagues did not doubt it was a bold Budget, and as such not without its risks. What impressed them, though, was the extent to which the Chancellor had already fulfilled the promise to cut tax on the nation's earnings which had been the central plank of their election platform. As he was leaving the meeting the present author asked the Chancellor what effect the 2 per cent jump in interest rates was calculated to have on the value of sterling on the foreign exchanges. 'What indeed?', was the enigmatic reply.

The restoration of incentives, and the concomitant shift from direct to indirect taxation, were but a part of the new Chancellor's break with the recent past. He also set about the dismantlement of artificial barriers to market functions with considerable relish. The Budget raised the foreign exchange allowance for travellers to £1000; the limit on property investment overseas to £100 000, and that on capital export-able by individuals to £200 000; and introduced automatic clearance of direct investment overseas up to £5m on a single project – all this as 'a first step'. This was swiftly followed in the autumn by the total abolition of exchange controls for the first time in almost 40 years.

This last move provoked a storm of protest. The Labour Opposition and the trades unions forecast that it would lead to a devastating drain of capital, which would otherwise have created jobs at home. It was a charge that was destined to be repeated with increasing fervour as overseas investment by British institutional funds duly gathered momentum over the next three and a half years. It was a move which essentially reflected a policy prejudice against market regulation. But the combination of sterling's emergence as a 'petrocurrency', a government whose commitment to vanquish inflation was taken at face value by the exchange markets, and high interest rates was leading to appreciation in the value of the pound to an extent which was already beginning to provoke expressions of anguish from British industry. Restriction on outward invest-ment had thus become an anomaly. Voices had been raised in favour of the reinforcement of controls on capital outflows with controls on inflows. Sir Geoffrey's decision to remove controls altogether was a more logical response – although hopes that this would lead swiftly to a softer rate for sterling were predictably confounded. The markets read the ending of controls as a bull signal for sterling, which rose higher.

The election manifesto had been cautious about the future of those other controls inherited from Labour, over prices and dividends. A 'review' was promised. That did not take long. As Parliament rose for the summer holidays the Price Commission was abolished. Its Chairman, Mr Charles Williams, was confident that the new government would soon learn the error of its ways: the previous Tory Government had also scrapped wage and price controls on taking office in 1970, only to reinstate them two years later. This time, however, there would be no second thoughts. Managements throughout the private sector were to be confronted with the unfettered opportunity to manage. It was not an opportunity that all would relish.

Old habits are slow to fade. In the late summer of 1979 the present author attended a conference with a number of senior managers from the private sector. Interest centred on the prospects for the winter pay round that lay ahead. The managing director of a private sector steel firm revealed that the figure he had written in his plans for wage increases was 16 per cent. Yet the steel industry was already facing intensifying competition from the new producers in the Third World. Was 16 per cent really the sort of increment to labour costs that such a business could sustain? 'Not remotely', was the disquieting reply. 'But that is going to be about the going rate for this winter's wage round, and it would be a waste of time for us to try and buck the trend.'

In this exchange was encapsulated a dilemma which had confronted successive governments for 20 years or more. The advocates of monetary control as the primary curb upon inflation argued that if cash were properly constrained across the total economy, both sides to wage bargaining in the private sector would come to see that excessive rises in unit labour costs must be self-defeating, since they could only lead to bankruptcy. They acknowledged that the application of such market disciplines to bargaining in the nationalised industries and public services would be more difficult, since access to the public purse removed the credibility of the threat of bankruptcy; and in most cases statutory monopoly eliminated equally the threat of loss of market. The logical solution lay, wherever practical, in privatisation and the elimination of monopoly: but this would take time where it was feasible at all. Meanwhile financial targets and cash limits would have to perform as substitutes for the forces of competition: hence the Chancellor's warning that cash limits would not accommodate the prospective rise in labour costs in public services, which would therefore have to be offset by economies in the numbers employed.

The sceptics – and they were well represented round the Cabinet table – had always argued that this approach was unrealistic. The unions in the public sector, where for the most part the labour force was subject to the discipline of the closed shop, would always seek to exploit the double privilege of monopoly and access to the public purse to extract exorbitant wage increases. These would be taken as the benchmark to be matched, at worst, by the unions in private industry. And there the threat of bankruptcy, though theoretically credible, would prove a broken reed. For businesses that were flourishing would concede large settlements rather than risk the loss through strike action of the customers flocking to their doors; while companies in trouble would calculate that if uncompetitive increases in their labour costs might eventually put them out of business, strikes called against refusal to concede such increases would put them out of business right away.

The sceptics had two alternatives to offer. One was legislation to restrict the immunities of trades unions; the other was some form of legalised restraint on collective bargaining. In 1979 even the sceptics round the Cabinet table could not forget – from personal experience – how legal controls on wage bargaining had laid the last Conservative Government low. Paradoxically the 1970 Tory manifesto had specifically rejected wage control, whereas the 1979 version had kept mum. Nevertheless there was no one in government in the summer of 1979 prepared to make the case for direct control of wages.

That did not alter the fact that the environment of wage bargaining which the government inherited was impregnated with the consequences of years of such control. Both sides of industry had become accustomed to operating within rules which tacitly disconnected what was paid from ability to pay it: rules based essentially on the concept of 'fairness' of reward for one form of employment *vis-à-vis* others. Hence it was not surprising that both sides of industry were going to enter the 1979 wage round assuming that what was paid in the public sector would determine what private firms would have to pay. Furthermore the years of wage control had dangerously eroded differentials, and thus thrown up strong pressure for their restitution; and because government had felt obliged to try to set an example of compliance with its own wage guidelines where it was itself the employer, and also because employees in the public services could not usually benefit from the sort of bogus 'productivity' schemes which the private sector had devised to get round pay restraint, pay in the public services had relatively lost ground. That, too, presaged ill with Professor Clegg and his Comparability Commission prowling like the hosts of Mideon.

The argument about trades union legislation cut across the usual lines of philosophy within the Tory Government and party.

The election manifesto had made more specific commitments in this area than in any other. 'We propose', it said, 'three changes which must be made at once': picketing to be restricted to the primary business in dispute; a right of appeal to be instituted for those dismissed through non-membership of a closed shop; and the provision of public funds to pay for secret ballots in union elections. It may be noted, however, that all of these changes were designed to protect the rights of individual union members. None of them was aimed at correction of what many in the business community believed to be the imbalance of power between the two sides of industry in wage bargaining. The furthest that the manifesto went in this direction was the promise of a 'review' to ensure that unions bore 'their fair share' of the cost of supporting members they called out on strike.

The modesty of these proposals reflected sharp divisions of opinion. Jim Prior made no secret of his scepticism about the scope for transforming Britain's industrial relations through changes to the statute book: what had appeared in the manifesto had represented, as far as he was concerned, inescapable sops to the strength of public feeling against union power. His scepticism was shared by John Biffen, usually classified at the other end of the party spectrum, although for different reasons. Jim Prior dreamed of a time when trades union leaders would socialise with him as freely and openly as they had done with Michael Foot, and was determined to prevent the erection of legislative barriers to the creation of such cheerful harmony. Biffen held no brief for that sort of corporatism; but he believed that the whole of experience of the Heath administration had proved conclusively the unwisdom of complex industrial relations legislation. Nigel Lawson, even more clearly identified with the opposite wing of the party to Jim Prior, shared Biffen's scepticism about the utility of industrial relations legislation as a mechanism for the control of inflation; although he supported changes in the law designed to make the union leaders more responsive to their members.

Against this viewpoint were ranged those who would usually have been seen as Jim Prior's natural allies: men like Ian Gilmour, Peter Walker and Michael Heseltine. Their profound scepticism, verging on contempt, towards 'monetarist economics', and their unreconstructed faith in the ability of government to oil the wheels of industry, obliged them to offer an alternative response to the challenge of inflation. That response was the legalised reform of industrial bargaining. They did not accept that the misfortunes which befell the Heath administration proved the impracticability of union legislation in the British context. On the contrary, they argued that had the Tory Government not been narrowly defeated in February 1974, the union leadership would have come to accept the 1971 Industrial Relations Act, whose provisions had indeed been widely welcomed by the union rank-and-file.

They had powerful allies in the Prime Minister and the

Chancellor. The Prime Minister warmed instinctively to the widespread popular demand, exacerbated by the miseries of early 1979, that the unions should be brought to heel. She viewed the wariness and reluctance of her Employment Secretary with unconcealed impatience. Sir Geoffrey Howe shared this impatience, and as a lawyer by training who had played a major role in shaping and carrying the 1971 Act, he could not accept that British trades unions should indefinitely regard the sort of legal restraints which were commonplace in Germany or the United States as a challenge to their manhood.

But it was Jim Prior who controlled the levers, and he was to prove more than a match for the activists. The commitments in the manifesto would be fulfilled; but that was as far as he would be prepared to move. Management would look in vain to government to stiffen its collective backbone with the statute book.

*   *   *

Before the ministerial team dispersed for their first summer holidays they had to receive the Treasury's midsummer 'medium-term economic assessment', and take their first look at future plans for public spending. The Treasury soothsayers had naught to offer for their comfort. They foresaw no likelihood of any real growth in the British economy for several years – over most of the lifetime of the new Parliament. Against such an unappealing prospect Sir Geoffrey Howe called upon his colleagues to hold public spending steady, since any growth would imply the need for higher taxes, higher interest rates or still more inflation. But the programmes which confronted them were not standing still. Reflecting Denis Healey's January White Paper, they were scheduled to grow by 2 per cent in volume: and on top of that there was the new government's own commitment to increase spending on defence by 3 per cent more than the rate of inflation, and to provide additional resources for the police. Under the circumstances the Cabinet's decision to limit any increase on the 1979–80 spending programmes to a maximum of £500m–£1000m, while it may not have reflected the Treasury's initial ambitions, nevertheless involved a commitment to finding economies of up to £4000m in 1980–1, which were reported to have provoked cries of anguish from Michael Heseltine and Mark Carlisle, Environment and Education Ministers respectively, whose departmental budgets seemed likely to bear the brunt of the Treasury axe. But this was, as always, a decision in principle: the real battles would take place after the holidays, when the Chief Secretary had to tailor the individual departmental spending plans. Decisions of principle by Cabinet were one thing: their practical application was something else again.

3 Settlement with Salisbury and Strife with Brussels

Mrs Thatcher is the sort of Prime Minister whom the Foreign Office think the gods have sent to try them. She is the first incumbent of 10 Downing Street since Neville Chamberlain to lead a government without previous experience of managing an external department – even Harold Wilson had been President of the Board of Trade. And she is, as they swiftly discovered, no Harold Wilson: what she lacked in personal experience she amply made up for in determination.

They had, however, a prize asset: had they been invited to choose a Foreign Secretary from the new ministerial team, they would surely have chosen Lord Carrington. As a former High Commissioner in Canberra, and Minister of Defence in the Heath administration, he was well known on the international circuit. Moreover, in the years of Opposition, he had shown his ability to influence and persuade a Leader who appeared to bear no rancour towards his aristocratic superciliousness in her regard. He patronised: like Ted Heath she seemed to like it.

The Foreign Office badly needed such an asset. For the new government confronted two major issues over which the Prime Minister's instinctive attitudes and Foreign Office intentions were flagrantly in contrast: Rhodesia and the Common Market.

Rhodesia had been a thorn in the flesh of the Tory Party ever since Mr Ian Smith declared his independence in 1965. The large majority of Tory MPs, reflecting the views of constituency activists, thought 'Smithy' was a good egg. From the start the Tory front bench, supported by a minority of the backbenchers, accepted that the Rhodesians, by seizing independence, were in rebellion against the Crown. Consequently when, with the

opening of the pheasant shooting season, trade sanctions
against Rhodesia fell to be renewed each year by Parliament,
the Tory front bench voted in favour, and there was a
backbench revolt: a small one when the Tory Party was in
government; a substantially larger one when it was in Opposition.

For years all this had been academic. Rhodesia survived
sanctions, and prospered. The British Government's claim to
exercise sovereignty over a rebel colony was at best a fiction and
at worst a joke. But in the middle 1970s circumstances
changed. The Portuguese, exhausted by the task of defending
their colonies of Angola and Mozambique, which flanked
Rhodesia on either side, against the opprobrium of the United
Nations, withdrew. Immediately Rhodesia was exposed to
guerrilla infiltration from all sides. By the end of 1978 the
Rhodesian army was losing the war. White Rhodesians,
confronted with an obligation to serve turn and turn about in
the armed forces well into middle age, had begun to take the
road to South Africa in increasing numbers. Those that
remained had agreed to a new constitution, giving full voting
rights to the black population, albeit with entrenched
safeguards for the white minority. Elections had been duly held
under the new constitution as Britain was going to the polls in
April. The Tory Party had despatched a team of observers,
which had given the elections their broad endorsement. A black
majority government, under Bishop Muzorewa, had been
returned to power. Mrs Thatcher, while still in Opposition,
had taken the occasion of a visit to Australia to indicate her
predisposition to accord formal recognition to the government
emerging from the April elections.

But the war continued, and the international community
showed no inclination to recognise a Rhodesian Government
which did not come 'from the muzzle of a gun', reflecting the
aspirations of one or other of the rival 'liberation' armies, led
respectively by Joshua Nkomo and Robert Mugabe. So the
freshly-installed Conservative Government faced a delicate
dilemma. If it persisted in the Prime Minister's professed
intention, withdrawing trade sanctions and recognising the
Muzorewa Government as the legally-constituted authority
over a sovereign Rhodesia, it would find itself in conflict with

the United Nations and the Commonwealth, which was due to hold a Prime Ministerial conference in Africa in July. Yet the new Prime Minister publicly predicted that there would not be a parliamentary majority for the renewal of sanctions come November. This was a pardonable exaggeration; since in the absence of an internationally acceptable settlement the Opposition parties would undoubtedly have supported the continuation of the sanctions, the likelihood of a parliamentary rejection was remote. But what was not remote was the likelihood of a profound and damaging rebellion in the Tory Party. So time was painfully short.

What ensued was widely interpreted as a triumph of British diplomacy, masterminded by those two patrician pragmatists, Lords Carrington and Soames, who had contrived to overcome the instincts and the public preferences of their Prime Minister and the majority of her backbenchers. At the Commonwealth Conference in Lusaka the Prime Minister was reluctantly persuaded to acknowledge publicly that legal independence for Rhodesia must be of a form to secure international endorsement, which Bishop Muzorewa was not going to receive. Salisbury got the message. A constitutional conference was assembled at Lancaster House in London, with the participation of both the guerrilla army leaders, as well as Ian Smith and Bishop Muzorewa. Rhodesia's 14-year-old 'rebellion' was formally abandoned, and Lord Soames was despatched as a twilight colonial governor, to be assisted by a British expeditionary force to supervise the disbandment of the guerrilla armies, and a posse of British electoral officials led by the former County Clerk of Cheshire to supervise some new elections.

Joshua Nkomo was widely tipped to win them. The Foreign Office, it was said, had consecrated him as Zimbabwe's first independent leader several years before, and Mr Tiny Rowland, Chairman of Lonrho and shrewd student of black African form, had his money on the Nkomo stable. Moreover Robert Mugabe was identified as a hard-line Moscow marxist, hand-in-glove with the Angolan regime of similar persuasion. Ian Smith and the South African Government by all accounts thought differently. The South Africans had found it possible to do business with the Angolans, and Ian Smith was openly scornful of Nkomo's prospects. To the consternation of the Foreign Office, they turned out to be correct. Mugabe won comfortably. Which was, perhaps, hardly surprising, since he represented the Shona, whereas Nkomo represented the Matabele; and there were a lot more Shona than Matabele in what was henceforth to be known as Zimbabwe. Tiny Rowland was not, by all accounts, the only one to be discomfited. The Prime Minister was said to be equally disenchanted by the poor form guide offered by our diplomats. Lord Soames, however, rose splendidly to the occasion. His generous hospitality and somewhat larger-than-life personality achieved an immediate rapport with Zimbabwe's first elected leader, and the Union Jack was hauled down in an atmosphere of mutual congratulation. Lord Soames returned to London to a hero's welcome and Mrs Thatcher on the tarmac.

Fleet Street rang with plaudits for the skill and ingenuity of the Foreign Secretary and the ephemeral colonial Governor. The Rhodesian embarrassment which had dogged the footsteps of successive British Governments for 14 years had been brilliantly resolved. Our last great colonial responsibility had been shed. The goal that had eluded Harold Wilson and Ted Heath, and Harold Wilson once again and Jim Callaghan, had finally been secured. The government was saved, in the nick of time, from an unholy row about trade sanctions. It was adjudged a rare feather in the government's cap – albeit one that had been achieved more in defiance of than in response to the Prime Minister's inclinations.

Four years later, with something akin to civil war raging in large areas of the former Rhodesia, and Joshua Nkomo temporarily in exile in London following threats to his life at home, Lord Soames was accustomed to recall the folly of those who had received Mugabe's victory as a victory for Communism. Nothing of the kind, he pointed out: it was a victory for the Shona tribe. Which was undoubtedly true, if rather rough on those who happened to come of a different bloodstock. But at least the British Parliament and Government were spared continuation of the obligation to assert a responsibility which they had lacked the power to exercise for 50 years. Like de Gaulle in Algeria, Lords Carrington and Soames had contrived to lance a boil. Their successful surgery owed more to time and opportunity than to superior wisdom by comparison with the surgeons who preceded them, and it was still a messy business. The world awarded its plaudits, which was what mattered.

*   *   *

Over Rhodesia the Prime Minister had effectively been outvoted by the Foreign Office. Over Europe she was to turn the tables. As in many other areas, the Tory Government had inherited burgeoning trouble. Britain's relations with the European Community were in need of attention. The preceding Labour Government had come to office in February 1974 profoundly split on British membership. The left of the Labour Party regarded the Community as a conspiracy to deny it the right to create socialism in one country; the right viewed it as at best a staging post on the road to the brotherhood of man. Harold Wilson had come up with a characteristic stratagem to keep his troops from fighting. Having roundly denounced a call from Mr Wedgwood Benn for a national referendum on the issue as unconstitutional, he then espoused the idea. But first he would 'renegotiate' new and better terms of membership to put before the nation. His partners did not take long to perceive that his concern was with appearances rather than substance, and wearily joined in his charade. Nothing of significance was conceded; but the Labour Leader was uninhibited in claiming that he had struck a new deal to put before the people. The people duly endorsed it, probably because those campaigning for confirmation of British membership of the Community had two high trumps in their hand: first, defence of the *status quo*, always the best position with British public opinion; and second, the unpopularity of the leading campaigners for a 'no' vote – Tony Wedgwood Benn and trades union leaders such as Jack Jones.

There followed a period during which, for fortuitous and largely climatic reasons (a series of poor world harvests), the budgetary costs of British membership had been modest. In 1975 we had even made a profit. But by 1978 the net cost of British membership was soaring to £800m; and according to Treasury figures published in the spring of 1979 it was not going to shrink. Furthermore, owing to the dismal performance of the British economy in the later 1970s, our income per head

had slid down to the poorest end of the Community membership, only undershot by the Italians and the Irish. The Labour
Government sulked, and in John Silkin it had found the ideal
spokesman for its sulkiness.

Participation in the Community had not visibly been an
issue in the 1979 election. Voters had other more domestic
matters on their minds; and while the Tory and Liberal Parties
were publicly committed to our continuing membership, they
sensed it was unlikely to carry many votes; whereas the Labour
Party saw it as an internally divisive topic which was best, if
possible, ignored.

Mrs Thatcher, however, shared enthusiastically – on this as
on most other issues – the majority Tory grassroots opinion.
The Community was taking us to the cleaners, and the Foreign
Office was doing next to nothing about it. This was going to
change.

The Treasury, which had to meet the bills for Community
membership, and instinctively disliked 'abroad' in any case,
was overjoyed. The Foreign Office was aghast. It did not burn
any candles for the common agricultural policy, which was
essentially responsible for the disproportionate costs we bore:
the Ministry of Agriculture was left to defend the CAP around
Whitehall single-handed. To the Foreign Office the CAP was a
classic fraud perpetrated by the French; and to the Foreign
Office the essential purpose of our membership of the Community was to score points off the French. But it also believed
that points were only to be scored off the French successfully in
alliance with the Germans (a forlorn hope, incidentally, as
repeated rebuffs should have taught them: but the Foreign
Office is blessedly unblemished by the scars of experience). The
new Prime Minister, by contrast, showed every inclination to
stamp on all our partners, including the Germans, in hobnailed
boots.

The skirmishing began in earnest within weeks of the
General Election. The new government rested its case upon the
provision in Britain's Treaty of Accession to the European
Community, negotiated by the Heath administration, according to which it was agreed that the terms and conditions of
British membership would be reviewed should an 'unacceptable situation arise'. The Brussels Commission promptly came

to Britain's aid with a report which confirmed that Britain was indeed among the poorest members of the club, and yet called upon to pay the heaviest subscription: and furthermore that this imbalance was expected to be accentuated in the years ahead.

Needless to say the French were entirely unimpressed. They argued plausibly that nothing had occurred which had not been, or at least should not have been, foreseen when Britain had decided to apply for membership. Since the British had a relatively tiny and efficient agricultural sector, they could never have expected to benefit much from the cost of Community agricultural support. Furthermore it was the British themselves who had insisted on preserving access to their markets for the farmers of New Zealand and the new Commonwealth, whose produce incurred Community levies on importation, which would not have been incurred by alternative imports from within the Community. They had therefore made their bed and had no right to complain of its discomfort. If Britain had failed to take advantage of access to the Community's markets for industrial goods, that was the consequence of fading British competitiveness, for which again we had no one but ourselves to blame. Besides, the United Kingdom now enjoyed the unique privilege of self-sufficiency in energy. At a time when other Community countries were struggling desperately to adjust to the second oil shock, the British were watching a huge windfall appreciation in the value of their oil reserves and sales.

In theory the new British Government faced a choice between three possible courses. It could go all out for a fundamental reform of the common agricultural policy to remove the causes of its high subscription. It could campaign for the introduction of major new Community expenditures on 'social' and 'regional' imbalances, from which our numerous industries in trouble could expect to benefit disproportionately, thereby cancelling out our disproportionate contributions to farm support. Or it could seek alleviation of its existing subscription costs.

Common sense might have pointed to adoption of the first course. As Community farming steadily advanced in productivity, the political desire to maintain and indeed improve farm incomes had resulted in the annual establishment of price guarantees at levels calculated to choke off domestic consumption, and hence in the accumulation of daunting surpluses of milk and dairy products, grain and wine and sugar beet, which had then to be dumped on world markets on the back of export subsidies. Yet most of the benefit of this profligacy did not flow to the peasant farmers of Southern France and Italy for whom it was theoretically intended, but to the wealthy barley barons of the Beauce and the Ile de France, and the efficient dairymen and bacon producers of Normandy, Holland and Denmark.

For a variety of reasons, however, Whitehall had lost faith in the scope for CAP reform. To the French the CAP was the ark of the covenant, and calls for reform were invariably interpreted in Paris as challenges to its very existence. The Germans, who had with Britain to foot the bill, seemed natural allies in the quest for reformation. But unfortunately the German agricultural sector was as inefficient as the German industrial sector was efficient. It included hundreds of thousands of weekend smallholders who were in reality employed in factories making cars and engineering products, but whose allegiance to the Christian Democrats and – even more important – the Liberal Free Democrats, who were usually indispensable to the formation of coalition governments in Bonn, was held to depend on their continued involvement in farming. For these people to show a proper sense of political gratitude, high farm prices were needed: and in fact it was the Germans, rather than the French, who had regularly demanded exorbitant annual increases in price guarantees. Moreover the annual Community farm price negotiation was conducted by the Ministers of Agriculture, who were invariably and collectively far more conscious of their answerability to the farmers than to the housewives.

So while CAP reform remained a pious aspiration for the Treasury (and not even that for the Ministry of Agriculture), it was not seen as practical politics. The second course – that of topping up Community spending on agriculture with new budgets for industrial and regional support – had many British advocates. The Foreign Office was inclined to regard it as likely to prove the least contentious and most *communautaire* escape route from the British budget problem. The Scottish, Welsh and Northern Ireland Offices were predictably enthusiastic, since they were likely to be the primary beneficiaries. The 'Europeans' in the Labour Party, the Liberals and many enthusiastic federalists in the Tory Party saw it as a means of giving the Community a new 'relaunch'.

Needless to say the Treasury was wholly unimpressed. It saw little attraction in supplementing massive subsidies for the weekend farmers of Bavaria with massive subsidies for worked-out British coalpits and hopelessly unproductive shipyards. Moreover it shrewdly reckoned that when it came to the point Britain would be required to foot still larger bills, while the wily continentals would be found to have collared the lion's share of the loot.

There was, however, another and more fundamental difficulty about the second course. The new Tory administration had come to office pledged to reduce the scale and cost of government and to cut the burdens of taxation. It would have been illogical, to put it mildly, for such a government to campaign for brand new bumper budgets for Brussels. That was most certainly the opinion of the Prime Minister, and the Foreign Office had rapidly, if regretfully, to concede that this was not a runner either.

So there was nothing for it but to fight for budgetary compensation. This had supposedly been promised under the 'renegotiated' terms of British membership of the Community agreed by Wilson and Callaghan in 1975. In practice, the 'corrective mechanism' had proved a broken reed. So before July was out Sir Geoffrey Howe was despatched to Brussels to serve notice that the new government expected the net cost of British contributions to the Community to be cut by £1000m a year. His reception ranged from frost to incredulity. A hard and bitter battle was in prospect.

As the autumn wore on Britain's partners came gradually and painfully to realise that they were dealing with a different sort of London Government to those they had been used to. The Heath administration had exhibited occasional spasms of Gaullist nationalism (at the time of the first oil 'shock' the then Prime Minister had seriously canvassed the possibility of diverting oil supplies in the hands of continental subsidiaries of British oil companies to the UK market). But in general it had been anxious to demonstrate 'community spirit'. After the farce of 'renegotiation' the Labour Government had for the most part withdrawn to its tent. Mrs Thatcher, it was discovered with dismay in the continental capitals, was out for her pound of flesh in deadly earnest. Nor were matters helped by the instant dislike which she and President Giscard d'Estaing took to each other. Although both led governments of a conservative complexion, they had nothing whatsoever in common. He was accustomed to refer to her as *'la fille de l'epicier'*; she to him as 'that bogus count'. Both were, of course, correct.

The climax effectively came at the Community summit in Dublin at the end of November. Mrs Thatcher was at her most hectoring and strident; 'it's our money' was her refrain. Tempers were not so much frayed as torn apart. The British diplomats were appalled, and the diplomatic correspondents of the British press, faithfully reflecting the shock and horror of their regular interlocutors, gave her savage notices. She had broken all the rules of international negotiation. She had alienated all sympathy for the British case. She had been offered a one-off rebate of £350m, and rejected it with contumely. This was no way to behave.

In reality it was to prove a well-judged performance. Ever since the days of General de Gaulle the Community had functioned ultimately on a basis of the reconciliation of respective national interests. Once, when his Foreign Minister had been complaining about Dutch intransigence, de Gaulle had pulled him up. 'The Dutch', he said 'are difficult people. They have a strongly-developed sense of self-interest. In short, a nation.' He would surely have regarded Mrs Thatcher as a woman after his own heart. As it was, her partners were nothing like as shocked as some of her officials. In the end they respected determination; and while nothing was settled in Dublin, the summit dispersed in the knowledge that something a good deal better than her partners' sighting offer was going to have to be forthcoming.

It took six more long weary months of tough negotiation to produce a settlement which the Prime Minister felt able to accept. But eventually at the end of May 1980 it was agreed that Britain would be refunded £1800m in respect of her budget contributions for 1980 and 1981, with provision for a third

year's repayment if a long-term solution to Community finance
had not been found by then. Mrs Thatcher had not got all she
had asked for. Britain's contribution of nearly £1000m in 1979
was uncovered, and there was no binding assurance of any
long-term solution. But she had undoubtedly recovered far
more than Whitehall had originally regarded as obtainable:
and in fact, owing to a slower growth of agricultural spending,
the British net contribution in 1981 was to drop almost to zero.
Meanwhile the Treasury was assured of a valuable contribution to its ambition to diminish government borrowing, and
payments which would otherwise have depressed our current
account were drastically reduced. Paradoxically the pound was
thereby given an extra underpinning just when British industry's distress about its strength was most vocal. No matter: to
the general public the Prime Minister had signally lived up to
her reputation as a doughty fighter for British national interests
– whatever the British diplomats might say behind her back.

4 Hard Pounding

The mood of the Tory Party faithful when they gathered for their first post-election conference in Blackpool in October 1979 was one of sobriety rather than one of celebration: the party managers had chosen the downbeat, not to say flatfooted, slogan of 'Realism and Responsibility'. In truth there was plenty to be sober about. Inflation, boosted by the continuing rapid rise in world oil prices and the Budget switch to indirect taxation, was accelerating into the high teens; and the Chancellor's hopes that employees would count the bottom line on their payslips after the cuts in taxation showed no sign of realisation. The engineering industry was locked in a crippling series of strikes for two days a week, and signs of resistance on the part of union members who had never been consulted were met with summary discipline by militant shop stewards. Employment was on a plateau, but there was every expectation that this was not going to last much longer. Government borrowing and the monetary aggregates were growing at rates which could not be reconciled with the targets set at Budget time without belief in miracles. The exchange rate for the pound had risen to $2.20, and over 90 (almost 50 per cent above its 1976 low point) on the index of currencies in which our trade was conducted. In times past this would have been hailed as an unimaginable restoration of international confidence in British economic management. But such is the perversity of human nature that it was now viewed with undisguised apprehension by the industrial boardrooms. At the annual conference organised by the CBI that body's director-general told them they were drinking in the 'last chance saloon': some of them were increasingly inclined to drown their sorrows while they could still afford to do so. Meanwhile Professor Clegg and his Comparability Commission were coming up with regular ajudications on pay in the public services. The reasoning behind them was not

51

always immediately apparent: but the profile that they cast of soaring labour costs was unmistakable. The message from the Prime Minister and her Chancellor at Blackpool, frequently repeated through that autumn, was that 'we cannot, and we will not, finance exaggerated settlements, whether in the public or the private sector'. Neither side of industry seemed inclined to take much notice.

Early in November the Prime Minister served warning, at the Lord Mayor's annual banquet, that the government would not hesitate to apply 'unpleasant and even painful remedies' to reverse the surge of inflation and monetary expansion; and what she had in mind soon materialised. On 17 November the Chancellor announced action intended to cut the current year's need to borrow from the £9000m reckoned to be in prospect back to the £8300m target in his first Budget: this was to be achieved by requiring North Sea oil companies to advance their payments of petroleum revenue tax by two months. But of far wider significance was the simultaneous announcement that the Bank of England's minimum lending rate was to be raised to 17 per cent: an unprecedented level, and substantially above prevailing market rates for money.

Also at the beginning of November the Chief Secretary, John Biffen, had unveiled his first Public Expenditure White Paper. It was a slim document whose scope was confined to the year beginning April 1980, and it reflected the outcome of the first of the new government's annual horse-trading sessions between the Treasury and the spending departments. The customary longer-term review of spending programmes was held over to the spring Budget, since there had not been time to look that far forward following the early summer election. But the shortened timescale of the first White Paper also, perhaps, reflected John Biffen's sceptical cast of mind, which made him instinctively wary of long-range planning.

Overall state spending in 1980–1 was to be held down to the level projected for the year in course. This was a demanding prospect. It involved a cut of some £3500m in the plans for 1980/1 that Denis Healey had bequeathed; yet within that, total defence spending was to rise by 3 per cent, and the provisions for law and order and the social services were also to go up. Hence other programmes had to make way, the weight of economies being demanded of them accentuated by the pace of the increase in labour costs in the public sector.

Even so there was perhaps an element of *leger-de-main* in the flat profile which John Biffen was able to present. For it was arrived at after allowance for £1000m-worth of sales of government shares in BP and forward sales of BNOC oil, which did not diminish state claims on the economy, and also for £750m of underspend by individual departments which might, or might not, materialise (although in fact it did – and more). Take those two items away, and state spending in 1980/1 was still planned to be some 4 per cent above the levels of Labour's last year in office. Small wonder, therefore, that the Prime Minister swiftly made it clear that the November 1979 White Paper was to be seen as very much of a preliminary canter.

Next came the so-called 'Industry Act forecast', giving the Treasury's view of prospects for the economy over the next twelve months. It made remarkably gloomy reading. Inflation was not expected to drop below 14 per cent, while output was expected to slump by 2 per cent. 'The implication', Parliament was told, 'is that there is likely to be some rise in unemployment.' That was widely seen as a remarkable understatement. The Chancellor declined to offer a prediction of what he would need to borrow in the next financial year. But he gave an indication of his preferences with dark warnings that unless public spending was more firmly restrained, and unless labour costs in the public sector moderated, taxes, which the Tories were still pledged to cut, might have to rise instead. John Biffen summed the prospect up – as usual with more candour than discretion – early in the New Year as 'three years of unparalleled austerity'.

Meanwhile developments on the industrial scene gave the government no comfort. The engineering employers had finally reached a settlement with the engineering union, after weeks of disruption which had ruinously weakened the industry's ability to survive the imminent recession, on terms which gave the union the substance of its demands, and in particular a pace-setting commitment to a phased reduction in the length of the basic working week. And at the turn of the year the British Steel Corporation entered a strike in which the union's demand for a 20 per cent increment 'with no strings' and the government's insistence that it would not provide the Corporation (which was already losing money on a daunting scale) with any additional cash to meet it, left no obvious room for compromise.

The strains were already beginning to show. The first parliamentary rebellion, led by a relatively senior and articulate backbencher, Julian Critchley, had been staged soon after Parliament's return from the summer holidays, against reductions in Foreign Office finance for BBC overseas broadcasting. In February, Critchley followed this up with a sharply-barbed critique of the Prime Minister's style and attitudes in the pages of the *Observer*. The effect was somewhat smothered by his attempt to cloak his views in anonymity – an attempt which was swiftly and predictably blown. Besides, the murmurs of Critchley and others could be attributed with some plausibility to disappointment that their talents had not won recognition and promotion.

Rumblings within the Cabinet were less easily brushed aside. While Critchley was writing in the *Observer* as 'a Conservative', Sir Ian Gilmour, Lord Privy Seal and long identified as the philosopher of the Tory left, was speaking in Cambridge about 'Conservatism'. The Prime Minister subsequently commented that there had been 'something for everyone' in Sir Ian's speech, and this was true. Nevertheless his warning that 'lectures on the ultimate beneficence of competition and on the dangers of interfering with market forces will not satisfy people who are in trouble' was widely seen as directed at some of his Cabinet colleagues, up to and including the Prime Minister.

There was a more embarrassing intervention from Jim Prior. Addressing a meeting of parliamentary journalists the Secretary for Employment made clear his view that Sir Charles Villiers, chairman of the Steel Corporation, was not up to his job and should go. It was by no means an unique opinion: many in Parliament and industry who did not remotely share Prior's emollient approach to industrial relations regarded Sir Charles as one of Harold Wilson's aberrations. But quite apart from the fact that a semi-public expression of no confidence in the chairman of a state corporation was an undoubted breach of normal Cabinet etiquette (the occasion was formally 'off the record'; but given the nature of the audience, the chances of confidentiality being observed were slight), at that particular moment it could not have been better calculated to undermine the Steel Corporation's unyielding stand in the steel strike. And in fact Jim Prior had made no secret of his view that to enter a major strike from a posture of inflexibility was fundamentally mistaken. 'You must have room to compromise', he had told the Tory backbenchers.

The Prime Minister's response to this gaffe was not, perhaps, best calculated to improve relations round the Cabinet table. Challenged by Robin Day in a television interview to sack her Employment Secretary, she replied that you did not sack a minister for a single error, and then added that Jim Prior was 'very, very sorry'. That he may have been: by all accounts he was also not best pleased by such a public reprimand.

In the event the steel strike dragged on for 13 weary weeks. It was marked by considerable violence, since although the steel union was not formally in dispute with the private sector steel firms, widespread mass picketing was used to bring them also to a halt. Jim Prior protested that this was precisely the sort of secondary action which his planned industrial relations legislation would be designed to regulate. But he declined to accelerate the implementation of his plans, arguing plausibly that legislation undertaken in haste was not unusually to be repented at leisure. His caution and reluctance were widely criticised in industry and upon his own backbenches: he was unrepentant.

The ultimate outcome of the strike was technically a victory for the union, in that Sir Keith Joseph was in the event induced to commit additional funds to the Steel Corporation to allow it to accept the terms of a settlement worked out by a three-man committee chaired by that eminent Labour fixer, Lord Lever. But it was indeed a pyrrhic victory. It was reckoned that it would take the employees of the Steel Corporation years to recoup, from the extra cash extracted by the strike, the earnings they had lost in its duration. There was nothing unusual about that. But in this case the strike led to a major and irreversible loss of market share. It also broke the authority of the union.

Before the strike had begun Sir Charles Villiers was asked to comment on suggestions that if it took place many of the Corporation's domestic customers would seek overseas supplies, and would not come back when it was over. 'Spread the word around', was his cheerful reply. 'It's not true, but I'm all for encouraging them to think it is.' In the event it turned out to be all too true. The most worrying aspect of the strike for the Steel Corporation and those whom it employed was that, notwithstanding the picketing of the private sector and the ports, British steel-using industries appeared to manage very well without it. Many of them vowed they would never rely on BSC as a 'single source' for their supplies again.

So Mr Sirs, the leader of the steelmen, was able to claim that the strike had won better terms for his members. How many tens of thousands of them owed their subsequent redundancy to his achievement is anyone's guess.

*   *   *

The 1979 Budget, and the autumn Public Expenditure White Paper, had inevitably confined their perspective to the foreground. In March 1980 Chancellor Howe and his Treasury colleagues were ready to present their plans for the lifetime of the Parliament. John Biffen's second public spending White Paper covered the four years to April 1984. But the real innovation was the publication of a 'Medium-term Financial Strategy', setting out the government's aims for the Budget deficit and for the growth of the key monetary indicator, sterling M3, over the same period.

First, however, the background and the immediate outlook incorporated in the traditional 'Budget judgement'. The Treasury calculated that national output had grown by about 1 per cent in 1979: less than enough, on the conventional reckoning, to avoid a rise in unemployment, but substantially better than a fall of $\frac{1}{2}$ per cent expected the previous June. However it was reckoned that since then output had been falling, and that in the first half of 1980 it would turn out about 2 per cent lower than a year previously. The UK's current payments had worked out considerably worse than expected, with a deficit of about £2500m reflecting both the weakness of manufactured export sales and the strength of manufactured import penetration. Inflation had risen to 16 per cent by the end of 1979, exactly as predicted, and was still rising. Government borrowing, at about £9000m, was reckoned to have been about £500m more than intended, notwithstanding the corrective action taken back in November. Monetary growth, at 12.1 per cent in the year to February, had been over the top of the target range notwithstanding the severity of interest rates.

Sir Geoffrey deduced that a 'broadly neutral' Budget was called for, to be struck from an increase in customs and excise duties worth £1200m, and an increase in tax allowances costing the same amount. But in addition, another £900m had been lopped off departmental spending programmes since the previous autumn's review.

The outcome of all this was expected to be a fall in output in 1980 'very tentatively' put at $2\frac{1}{2}$ per cent, with inflation still hovering around 16 per cent by the year's end, and only falling thereafter to 13–14 per cent by mid-1981, while the current account was expected to show but a modest improvement, to a deficit of £2250m. The Budget deficit was put at £8500m, somewhat less than the expected 1979/80 outturn, although slightly more than the Budget forecast for that year; and money growth was put at 9 per cent.

The Chancellor made no attempt to hide the sombre nature of this prospect, which clearly presaged a steep rise in unemployment. This, he explained, 'is partly the consequence of a poor projected real trade balance, reflecting both weak world demand and the effects of a rate of inflation in the United Kingdom in excess of the money supply target. The second major factor is a likely swing from positive to negative stockbuilding.' In other words, it was essentially a reflection of lost competitiveness, and the sluggishness of labour market response to monetary disciplines.

It was therefore a propitious moment, perhaps, to concentrate the public gaze upon the far horizons. The flight path which the Chancellor described, and which the Chief Secretary confirmed in his White Paper, was a path to virtue. State spending, effectively unchanged in the year ahead, would thereafter fall steadily, both absolutely and as a proportion of national resources. Since receipts meantime would rise, the prospect was held out of a very handsome dividend of tax reliefs in what was likely to be the next election year. Against this background monetary growth would shrink steadily from year to year, leading to very low inflation at levels unexperienced since the early 1960s.

All this was naturally dismissed by the conventional critics as a 'monetary straitjacket' for an economy suffering from acute internal haemorrhage. More pertinently, perhaps, the profile of public expenditure aroused disbelief – even ridicule – in one particular. This was the calculation, central to the arithmetic of the whole exercise, that the nationalised industries, which in 1979–80 had needed £2300m from the government to keep going, would by 1983 be net repayers to the Treasury to the tune of £400m. This was deemed to imply a rise in their prices of a scale which no government would swallow, as well as a turnaround in their performance which flew in the face of all experience.

Be that as it may, the philosophy and the purpose behind the medium-term financial strategy were summed up in one phrase in the 'Red Book' issued on Budget Day, and a passage in the Treasury's covering note to the Commons Select Committee on the Treasury and Civil Service. 'Control of the money supply will', stated the Red Book, 'over a period of years reduce the rate of inflation. The speed with which inflation falls will depend crucially on expectations both within the United Kingdom and overseas.'

> The Government [said the Treasury memorandum] has deliberately not set its targets in terms of the ultimate objectives of price stability and high output and employment because these are not within its direct control. It has instead set a target for the growth of the money supply, which is more directly under its influence, and has stated that it will frame its policies for taxation and public expenditure to secure a deceleration of money supply without excessive reliance on interest rates.

In these two passages was encapsulated the whole nature of the Thatcher Government's break with the traditions of postwar economic management in Britain. Monetary targets were far from new. They had first been set by Roy Jenkins as a Labour Chancellor in 1968; and having been effectively allowed to lapse by his Tory successor, Tony Barber, in 1972, had been reasserted by Denis Healey at the end of 1976, and maintained ever since. But in 1968, and again in 1976, they had been imposed upon reluctant Labour Governments by their international creditors. Furthermore they had always been presented as adjuncts to the conventional yardsticks of governmental performance, which had been full employment and output growth; and they had been accompanied by attempts to restrain domestic inflation through centralised control of wage bargaining.

In practice growth had been sluggish, and when it had accelerated, as in 1973, it had been accompanied by much more rapid and unsustainable inflation; while the goal of full employment had steadily receded. Nevertheless the postwar convention that expansion and full employment were at the government's command had been respected; and monetary control had been treated as an alien discipline to which lip-service must be paid to appease the financial markets (and our creditors when, as regularly occurred, they were in the driving seat).

The medium-term financial strategy espoused a wholly different concept. It formally abandoned the pretence that full employment and economic growth were in the gift of government, accepting by implication that the achievement of these desirable objectives depended on the ability of British commerce to meet the appetites of its customers at home and abroad. It did not even promise a smart return to price stability, even though this was evidently the goal. Instead it set its sights on targets which were more directly within the power of government to influence: monetary growth and public borrowing. The implication was that if negotiators in the market place continued to behave as they had grown accustomed to, seeking to beat past inflation and to keep up with their neighbours, regardless of the performance of the sectors in which they happened to work, they would price themselves out of employment: and that this would apply in the public corporations and services through cash control of spending programmes and government lending just as it would apply in private industry through loss of market share. But because the government had served notice of its intentions towards the amount of cash in circulation, and the course of public spending, the hope was that negotiators would adjust their conduct to the new environment, and in that case the abatement of inflation would be achieved with minimum sacrifice of employment and services. It was very much as if the emperor had himself acknowledged the scantiness of his wardrobe. Needless to say this was widely interpreted as an affront to public decency (not least by those who had been accustomed to denounce politicians for arousing unsustainable expectations).

The architect of this striking adjustment to policy objectives was not the Chancellor of the Exchequer. To a remarkable extent the medium-term financial strategy was the brainchild of a second-rank Treasury Minister, the Financial Secretary Nigel Lawson. To the paternalistic interventionist school of Tory politics within the Cabinet – to the Priors and Gilmours, Carringtons and Walkers – it constituted an abdication of responsibility which, with luck, would pass, as 'reality' and lost by-elections made their impact. But it was also opposed from a rather different standpoint by the Chief Secretary, John Biffen. Biffen certainly had no faith in the capacity of governments to put everyone to work or capture markets; but he was equally sceptical about their ability to stick by a long-term programme of monetary and public expenditure objectives. Lawson, however, pursued his purpose with single-minded determination. The Chancellor, confronted by profound scepticism on the one side, and zealous determination on the other, found the zeal more persuasive, or at the least less easily resistible.

It cannot be said that either of the two key instruments emphasised in the medium-term financial strategy – monetary control and public spending – proved rapidly responsive. Back in the early 1970s the chief economic adviser to the Bank of England, Mr Charles Goodhart, had propounded what had subsequently become known as 'Goodhart's Law': that the performance of any monetary statistic selected as a thermometer to the economic temperature would be distorted as a result of its selection. A signal vindication of Goodhart's Law was at hand.

Since 1978, as already noted, quantitative controls on bank deposits, known as 'the corset', had been applied by the Bank of England in an effort to restrain lending by the High Street banks. The 'corset' did wonders to the performance of the sterling M3 target indicator which the Thatcher Government had inherited from Denis Healey. But as its sobriquet implied, it did so by displacing the evidence of fat rather than by eliminating the excess avoirdupois. This displacement had been facilitated by the abolition of exchange controls, so that by the summer of 1980 the illogicality of the corset had become a matter of comment in the City.

In July the Bank of England took the hint and unlaced the corset. The consequence was awful to behold. In the first three months of the financial year sterling M3 had been recorded as growing at an annual rate of 11–12 per cent: over the top of the Chancellor's chosen target range, but not so far over as to invalidate all hopes of bringing it back on course before the year was out, and of course far below the going rate of inflation. But when the figures for July were released early in August it was revealed that without benefit of corset the rate of growth in money had been almost twice as fast as hitherto believed: in fact significantly *faster* than inflation.

The figures were greeted by gasps of embarrassment or indignation. All sorts of extenuating circumstances were adduced: it was emphasised that just as the corset had artificially compressed £M3 growth while it had been in operation, its removal artificially inflated it; it was pointed out that other monetary aggregates – the narrower M1, the broader PSL 1 and 2 – were far better behaved. All of which was true, but did not altogether remove the angst. The government's real mistake had been its failure to remove the corset on taking office. The resulting spectacle could then have been fairly blamed on Denis Healey who, with superb insouciance, announced that he had 'never known such incompetence in my whole life'.

More to the point, the Prime Minister was dismayed. The Governor of the Bank of England was invited to 10 Downing Street for urgent explanations. Since both he and the Deputy Governor turned out to be unavailable, the lot fell instead on the number three in the Bank, John Forde. By all accounts it was a painful interview – so painful, indeed, that Mr Forde was said to have aged by several years in the space of as many hours. From the American prophet of monetary management, Milton

Friedman, downwards, there were numerous comments that the Prime Minister's whole strategy was being undermined by the incompetence of the central bank. It was a view the Prime Minister herself was known to share. Relations between Downing Street and Throgmorton Street were icy. Hugh Gaitskell had once said that while the Treasury displayed loyalty without expertise, the Bank displayed expertise without loyalty. That was a backhanded compliment to the Bank which the government in 1980 would not have paid.

Nor was the other proximate instrument chosen by the government for economic management, public spending, proving more responsive. The spring White Paper had identified the nationalised industries as the area where the most dramatic turnaround in public finances was to occur. So far they were showing every sign of progressing in the opposite direction. For while the administration in general, and the Prime Minister and Sir Keith Joseph, the Industry Secretary, in particular, were often charged with a philosophical bias against the nationalised industries – a charge to which they would have happily pleaded guilty – in practice the claims of the public corporations often proved as irresistible as they had done in the past. Once, when the Prime Minister was preparing an important speech, she demanded a fierce passage about the profligate abuse of public funds by the state businesses. She was hastily reminded by one of her civil servants that some hours before she was due to speak additional finance was to be announced for one of them. 'That', she replied, 'is precisely what I mean.'

Alfred Herbert, largest of the domestic machine tool manufacturers, rescued by Mr Wedgwood Benn from bankruptcy in the middle 1970s against official advice, was allowed to pass into receivership; and the Meriden motorcycle cooperative, once Mr Wedgwood Benn's pride and joy, was refused a write-off of its debts to government which had been demanded as the precondition for another rescue deal. But no attempt was made to foreclose upon it in the light of its inability to service the debt; and on a larger scale Harland and Wolff, the Belfast shipbuilders into which more than £100m of taxpayer funds had been injected since 1975, having been told to mend its ways or else in 1979, and having failed very obviously to do so, was provided with another £42½m in the summer of 1980 to keep it going. Rolls-Royce 1971, nationalised by the previous Tory Government after passing into receivership, announced losses of £58m in respect of 1979, and was reported to be needing to raise £200m backed by government guarantee (it could hardly have hoped to raise anything at all without one). British Leyland had, after considerable heart-searching, been provided with a further £300m in December 1979, with the promise of an additional £130m over the period 1981–3, and this was already looking quite inadequate. De Lorean, perhaps the most improbable of all the industrial speculations perpetrated by the Callaghan Government, ultimately doomed all too predictably to end in farce, was topped up with compensation for inflation. Inmos, a sort of throwback to Harold Wilson's white heat of technological revolution, a microchip manufacturer operating out of California (albeit with the promise of eventual establishment in the UK) and patronised and substantially financed by the Callaghan administration, was, after lengthy agonising, granted an extra £25m.

Among the public corporations proper, the Gas Corporation announced a pretax profit (on a partial current cost accounting basis) of more than £400m for 1979–80, and following the recommendations of one of the last reports from the Price Commission in the summer of 1979, was committed by the government to raising its prices by 10 per cent more than the rate of inflation over each of the next three years, presaging even more impressive profits in the future – albeit at the expense of its captive customers. From the Treasury's viewpoint its performance shone out like a good deed in a naughty world. The Post Office announced a profit of £175m before exceptional items; but this was half the profit made in 1978/9. The Coal Board had lost almost £160m (admittedly this was precisely on target); the electricity boards had produced a paltry surplus of £37m – and had had to be authorised to borrow an extra £300m to stockpile coal it did not need but for which the Coal Board had to have a buyer. British Rail, after allowing for the grants it got for running 'social' services, had drifted into the red. British Shipbuilders had produced a record deficit of over £150m, notwithstanding the subsidies it received from Whitehall to enable it to compete with quotes from foreign shipyards. As for the Steel Corporation, it had comfortably exceeded the government's worst expectations with a pretax loss of almost £550m, with the government driven to abandon its external financing limit.

Apart from British Gas, which basked in the privileged position of monopoly purchaser of North Sea gas at a bargain basement price, and which was now catching up on years of government-dictated subsidisation of its domestic customers, the managements of the nationalised industries blamed their performance – with some justice – on the recession. This was scant comfort to the private sector, which had no consoling access to the public purse. Here events were moving with dramatic speed.

Within one month of Sir Geoffrey's second Budget, orders for manufacturing industry had, in the words of one CBI leader, 'fallen off a cliff'. Export deliveries were so far proving resilient notwithstanding the steady appreciation of the pound, although manufacturers were becoming strident in their warnings that the prices they were able to command abroad were forcing them to contemplate wholesale withdrawal from major foreign markets. But home orders were collapsing. The Central Statistical Office calculated that British industry had cut its stocks more drastically in the first quarter of the year than at any time since records had first been compiled in 1955; and in June the Birmingham Chamber of Commerce reported that in the heartland of British engineering and metal manufacture output had slumped by 25 per cent in just three months. Unemployment, which had remained on the plateau to the end of 1979, had begun to accelerate dramatically, with the 'headline' figure jumping by 100 000 in June, and by 200 000 in July, and no prospect of any easement in sight. Inflation had finally peaked at an annual rate of 21 per cent in June, and July produced a sharp drop to under 17 per cent; but since this reflected no more than the absence of a repetition of the jump in VAT in 1979, further progress was not expected to be swift. And earnings – up 22 per cent in the year to August – were still rising even faster, and thus continuing to eat into what was left of profit margins. Commenting on the CBI's July survey of members' sentiment, which reported that more than half the respondents had shed labour in the previous four months, while

61 per cent were expecting to do so, the chairman of the Confederation's economic committee described it as 'as gloomy a picture as it is possible for anyone to paint . . . and I fear things will get worse before they get better'.

Understandably, therefore, when the great men of British industry gathered in Brighton for the CBI's annual autumn conference, the mood had overtones of panic. Terence Beckett, the newly-appointed director-general, spoke of a 'bare-knuckle fight' to get industry's clamour for a sweeping cut in interest rates and the exchange rate through to government. Sir Michael Edwardes, the embattled head of British Leyland, complaining bitterly that industry and commerce were being strangled by the pressures of a petrocurrency, told the Cabinet that if it 'cannot find a way of living with North Sea oil, then I say leave the bloody stuff in the ground'.

Yet the heady seaside rhetoric soon evaporated. Early in the following week Terence Beckett and his President paid a call on the Prime Minister in Downing Street. The press corps, assembled to greet them as they emerged from Number 10, expected to see the signs of bloody battle on their hands. So it came as something of a let-down to be told that there were, after all, no bounds to the faith and confidence placed by the captains of industry in the Prime Minister and her government.

5 Upstairs, Downstairs

Unlike its predecessor in 1970, the Thatcher administration did not come to office with a blueprint for major reform of the central machinery of government in its knapsack. Prior to 1970 Mr Heath had, in Opposition, masterminded a complex and detailed study of the machinery of government, involving among other things a number of information-gathering visits to Washington to see what we could learn from American ideas. On taking office, he and his ministerial team had set to work with a will; and over the ensuing three years Whitehall had been subjected to perhaps its heaviest upheaval since the war. The entire system of local government had been redrawn by Peter Walker; and that of the National Health Service by Sir Keith Joseph. The Central Policy Review Staff, or 'Think Tank', had been set up to provide the Cabinet with an independent, non-departmental watchdog of its strategy. Brand new 'super-departments', of Environment and of Trade and Industry had been created (plus another for Energy in the wake of the first 'oil shock' in 1973). Some functions – procurement for the Ministry of Defence, property management for government in general – had been 'hived off' into special agencies. Sophisticated new control techniques – 'PPBS' (programme, planning, budgeting systems) and 'PAR' (programme analysis and review) – had been introduced to cross-check on what Whitehall was up to.

Inevitably, perhaps, in the aftermath of the electoral defeats of 1974, there was considerable revulsion within the Tory Party against this whole approach. The reform of local government and of the Health Service were widely regarded as expensive flops; and the innovations in the central machinery of government were condemned for having resulted, not in streamlining, or the elimination of waste, but rather in additional bureaucracy.

So Mrs Thatcher would have been greeted with dismay inside her party had she shown any inclination to follow in her predecessor's footsteps. But she had none. If Ted Heath approached Whitehall with the zest of a mechanic confronted with a complex but creaking engine, his successor approached it with something not so far removed from bloodlust in her eye. She was no respecter of civil servants, sharing the conviction of many of her followers that over the years they had grown sleek, lazy and obstructive at the expense of the taxpayer and private enterprise. They, for their part, soon came to see her as abrasive, interfering and prejudiced. It was an unsettling relationship.

One of the first actions of the new government was to declare a three-month moratorium on civil service recruitment. Thereafter all departments were invited to consider and report back on the consequences of economies of 10 per cent, 15 per cent and 20 per cent in manpower. Unsurprisingly, without exception they reported that even 10 per cent would mean the end of life as we knew it. So by early 1980 a less draconian medium-term programme of manpower economies, designed to reduce the civil service by 100 000 over four years, was unveiled. At the same time Sir Derek Rayner, a senior executive from Marks and Spencer who had been recruited by Ted Heath to launch the Procurement Agency, was called back to mastermind a series of trawls for savings through Whitehall.

Progress was uneven. Thanks in large part to the moratorium, civil service numbers fell by no less than 20 000 in the first four months after the General Election. But there was an element of artificiality about this flying start; and in the following spring the Commons Select Committee on the Civil Service revealed in suitably shocked tones that the staff provision in the 1980/1 estimates for the civil service was actually higher than that for the previous year. This revelation proved to be misleading on the other side: it reflected in part a reclassification of catering staff. Nevertheless the disbelief with which the Select Committee greeted the assurance from Lord Soames (who had been somewhat improbably rewarded for his triumph in Rhodesia with the civil service to look after) that 'the general trend from now on will continue to be downwards' was widely shared.

In fact it proved misplaced. By February 1983, Barney Hayhoe, Treasury Minister of State with responsibility for the civil service, was able to announce that numbers had already shrunk by 80 000 since the government took office. The Prime Minister's commitment to achieve the smallest civil service since the last war was on course to fulfilment.

The so-called 'Rayner scrutinies' met with rather more mixed fortunes. Over the lifetime of the 1979 Parliament more than 150 of these specialist reviews of Whitehall procedures were either completed or commissioned, and savings in excess of £200m were reckoned to have emerged from them. But some of the most important fell by the wayside. A proposal that substantial economies could be achieved by encouraging pensioners and other recipients of weekly benefits through the Post Office to opt for payment through their banks or savings accounts was successfully aborted by a well-orchestrated lobby of sub-Post Offices, which stood to lose a lot of business, particularly in country areas usually represented by Tory MPs. Another proposal, that those who wished to clear their goods, and even perhaps their persons, through customs outside normal working hours should be required to meet the full cost to HM Customs of providing staff to enable them to do so, met combined resistance from the Departments of Trade, Industry and Transport and the regional departments. More funda-mentally some critics – notably Leslie Chapman, a former civil servant who had published a remarkable exposé of bureau-cratic resistance to labour-saving in the 1970s – argued that the civil service had 'domesticated' Rayner and his scrutineers (who were drawn from Whitehall). But probably the most effective defensive mechanism of the bureaucracy, both in Whitehall and in the town halls, was what was dubbed the 'bleeding stump syndrome': the selection for precedence of those candidates for retrenchment which would cause the maximum political embarrassment.

Another corner of the public payroll which had attracted considerable attention in the Tory Party in the days of Opposition were the so-called 'quangos' or 'quasi-non-governmental organisations'. Philip Holland, the Tory MP for Carlton, had produced a report recommending wholesale dismantlement of these bodies, which covered a multitude of activities, ranging from those like the Arts and Sports Councils which distributed public patronage, through advisory bodies such as the Parole Board to tribunals such as those which adjudicate over contested claims for supplementary benefits or the level of rents. According to a White Paper published in 1979 there were upwards of 2000 of these institutions, costing some £6800m a year. An eminent former Treasury civil servant, Sir Leo Pliatsky, was entrusted with the task of reviewing their dispensability. The outcome was a modest shaving. Some 440 were weeded out: but 46 new ones were added to the list; and the total saving amounted to less than £100m a year.

The aspect of bureaucracy which had generated most heat in the years of Opposition, however, had been the entitlement of the overwhelming majority of those employed directly or indirectly by the state to pensions whose value was automatically adjusted each autumn to take account of the rise in prices over the preceding 12 months. This privilege had been instituted by the Heath Government in 1971 following a long campaign spearheaded by the armed forces pensioners, who tended to be powerfully represented in Tory constituency associations. As inflation gathered momentum in the 1970s resentment had grown apace among those in the private sector, whose employers could not normally risk entering into such an open-ended commitment, and who yet had to contribute through the tax system to bridging the gap between what serving public servants contributed and what turned out to be the cost of pension provision. Yet it was a delicate grievance for government to respond to. The number of beneficiaries of index-linked pensions was large and growing all the time; and since serving public servants had had their annual wage settlements 'abated' throughout the 1970s by the government actuary's assessment of their appropriate pension contribution, action now to cut off or diminish inflation compensation would inevitably involve a retrospective adjustment to their terms of employment.

As usually happens when governments are confronted with a delicate grievance, resort was had to a Committee of Enquiry. Chaired by a leading industrialist, the ex-chairman of Lucas Industries, Sir Bernard Scott, this Committee reported in the autumn of 1980 in terms which hardly corresponded to the expectations of private sector critics, Tory backbenchers, or for that matter the Prime Minister. In general it concluded that instead of withdrawing index-linked pension entitlement from the public sector workforce, the government should contrive to extend it to the private sector. How this feat was to be financed in the downward slope of an exceptionally severe recession it did not bother to explain.

The Scott Report was, understandably, allowed to gather dust. Instead the government bent its mind to devising ways of increasing the contribution – whether actual, or notional in terms of 'abatement' – to be paid by serving public servants to the cost of their pensions. But here, too, there were formidable obstacles: for there was an obvious danger that enhanced contributions would in practice have to be offset by larger pay awards when government policy was aimed at holding down the public sector wage bill. Fortunately as the inflationary tide receded, so did hostility to the public pension privilege; and in the end the conundrum was passed on to the next Parliament unresolved.

Another piece of uncompleted business which exercised the mind of government in the summer of 1980 was the future of the Clegg Comparability Commission. As already mentioned, the new administration had undertaken to abide by its findings, although like the Labour Government it had also warned that resulting salary increases in public services would have to be paid for within the predetermined cash limits. Even so, the Commission's deliberations produced horrendous results: civil service pay – inflated, it is true, by the fortuitous timing of awards – shot up by 25 per cent between 1979 and 1980. Moreover some of the Clegg recommendations seemed, to put it mildly, idiosyncratic. Having been advised by management consultants that the trainers of chiropodists, occupational therapists and the like in the NHS were being paid 17 per cent more than those in comparable employment in the private sector, and having apparently accepted that advice, the Commission went straight on to recommend that these worthies should be paid another 12 per cent. Then, in May, the Commission was caught out (by the *Sunday Telegraph*) in a simple mathematical error. According to its own sums – their figuring based in any case on not much more than thin air – it should have recommended an increase of 9 per cent for teachers. Instead it had recommended 13 per cent – at an extra cost of £130m. Professor Clegg still retained some admirers on the government benches, led by Jim Prior. But they looked increasingly besieged, and before Parliament rose for its summer holidays the Prime Minister announced that the Commission was to go.

'Of course', the Professor commented morosely, 'our rewards have fuelled inflation. That has nothing to do with us. That has to do with what happened before. The public sector was held back by the Labour Government. In those circumstances, if we were to do the job properly, the result was inevitable.' But the Professor, like others before him, confidently predicted that it would not be long before the government found they could not do without a body such as his.

* * *

Thus the government gradually, and by sometimes halting steps, asserted its authority and influence over those who ran the state machine. It was equally gradualist in its approach to the machine itself. An illuminating point of conflict which took the best part of two years to resolve concerned the future of the Civil Service Department.

The CSD was to all intents the brainchild of Lord Crowther-Hunt, an Oxford crony of Harold Wilson's who had drafted the report of the Fulton Royal Commission into the Civil Service in the 1960s. Previously the civil service had been run from within the Treasury. The years that followed the establishment of the CSD had witnessed a dramatic upsurge in both the numbers and the cost of the bureaucracy: in the eyes of many Conservatives, and not least those of the Prime Minister herself, the two developments were not entirely unconnected.

The debate about the future of the Civil Service Department was, to an unusual extent for British Government, conducted in public. The Commons Civil Service Select Committee embarked upon an investigation, to which the head of the civil service, the Secretary to the Cabinet and Sir Derek Rayner gave conflicting evidence. The head of the civil service, Sir Ian Bancroft, argued forcefully that the management of Whitehall was more than any modern Chancellor and Treasury Permanent Secretary could cope with. His arguments were strongly supported by his predecessor Lord Armstrong, formerly Ted Heath's indispensable Man Friday, and now Chairman of the Midland Bank. They were vigorously contested by Sir Derek Rayner, and rather more cautiously by Sir Robert Armstrong, Secretary to the Cabinet.

The Select Committee found in favour of Sir Derek and Sir Robert. A fierce struggle ensued behind closed doors in Whitehall, from which Sir Ian Bancroft emerged victorious. The CSD was reprieved notwithstanding the Prime Minister's own well-known doubts. But not for long. There followed the six months' industrial dispute which was to disrupt tax-gathering throughout the early part of 1981. When it was over the earlier decision was reversed. The CSD was brought back into the Treasury after all.

It did not, however, altogether lose its identity. A Management and Personnel Office was set up with its own Cabinet Minister (Lady Young) in charge, and while the former Commons spokesman for the Department, Barney Hayhoe, was converted into a Treasury Minister of State, he retained his separate slot at Commons question time, and for many months continued to preside over the former department's premises on the Mall. It was, in short, rather more of a merger than a takeover. And the crucial Treasury oversight of promotion in the highest echelons of Whitehall, which Fulton had eliminated, was not restored.

This was to be the only major departmental reorganisation in the lifetime of the first Thatcher administration. Sir Keith Joseph toyed with plans to merge his Department of Industry with that of Trade once more (the linkage had been severed by Harold Wilson in 1974 to clip the wings of Tony Wedgwood Benn). Characteristically, Sir Keith's ambition was to have the interventionist Industry Department absorbed by the more market-orientated Department of Trade. His senior mandarins – and first and foremost his Permanent Under-Secretary, Sir Peter Carey – had other ideas. The merger did not happen (and when eventually it did, following the 1983 General Election, it was Industry which came out on top).

In the early months of the new government, Whitehall-watchers claimed to detect Prime Ministerial distaste for the system of Cabinet Committees which, in recent years, had proliferated as the scope and interests of government had grown beyond the capacity of Cabinet itself to handle them. The Prime Minister was said to feel that the parallel system of committees of officials which shadowed the Cabinet Committees of Ministers had grown to preempt too many choices and rig too many decisions. There was in fact little evidence to substantiate this bias in the Prime Minister's approach. Certainly ministers swiftly learnt to negotiate with her in *tête-à-tête* whenever problems of potential public conflict confronted them. But there was nothing new to that: winning the Prime Minister's ear has been an indispensable skill for British departmental ministers to learn from time immemorial. And in fact Mrs Thatcher introduced an important new dimension to the Cabinet Committee system, with a small committee of senior ministers (the so-called 'Star Chamber') established under Willie Whitelaw to act as arbiter between the Treasury and the spending departments when, as increasingly occurred, they were unable to resolve their differences in bilateral negotiations.

That is not to say that the Prime Minister's approach to her office was traditional. It was nothing of the kind. Traditionally the Prime Minister, absolved from responsibility for policy initiation, which rests with individual departmental ministers, is the arbiter whose powers of patronage ensure that their backing will enable one minister or department to prevail against another, and occasionally the inspiration which can shift the inertia of Whitehall and move the whole machine in a new direction. For Mrs Thatcher arbitration had no appeal. Armed with a constitution which enabled her to work almost around the clock, and a grasp of departmental briefs which rapidly became legendary, there were few backwaters of government too remote to escape her interest and attention. Yet she remained astonishingly detached. She often spoke in private, and occasionally in public, as if she were a backbench critic rather than the Queen's First Minister. Her impatience with Jim Prior's gradualist approach to industrial relations reform, the Foreign Office's preoccupation with international goodwill, the Department of Industry's softness of touch by businesses in trouble, or the reluctance of the Home Office to give satisfaction to the Tory critics of immigration and crime prevention policies, was notorious. It was not unknown for her to compliment backbenchers on organising revolts which the ministerial vote had been mustered to defeat.

Yet she was in no hurry to mould a government more obviously attuned to her own priorities. Eighteen months were to elapse before the first ministerial reshuffle. Nor did she take steps to strengthen centralised control of Whitehall from 10 Downing Street. She followed Callaghan's example in assembling a tiny political 'Think Tank', consisting of John Hoskyns, a successful entrepreneur who had sold his own computer software business and then volunteered his services to Sir Keith Joseph in Opposition, and Norman Strauss, another recruit from the private sector, to double-bank the Central Policy Review Staff. But while the CPRS did not begin to recapture the role it had enjoyed under the last Conservative administration, it is doubtful whether Hoskyns and Strauss had as much influence on actual policy formulation as their predecessor Dr Bernard Donoghue had enjoyed with Jim Callaghan. Later, in 1981, the in-house team at Number 10 was reinforced by the arrival of Professor Alan Walters, a monetarist economist who established a close and effective working relationship with the Prime Minister and (after a period of considerable tension) also with the Treasury, and powerfully influenced the Prime Minister's thinking, not only in economic policy, but also towards the nationalised industries.

It was alleged that the Prime Minister sought to 'politicise' the civil service, by reserving promotion to the highest posts for those who shared her own priorities. There was little evidence to sustain this allegation either. Sir Douglas Wass, a natural agnostic in the conflict between the Keynesians and monetarists, but one whose own background and personal connections leaned more to the former than the latter, survived until retirement as Permanent Secretary to the Treasury almost to the end of the Parliament. Sir Frank Cooper, whose capacity to defend the budget of the Ministry of Defence against the challenges of the Treasury earned him the designation as the 'marmalade mafia', survived when his ministers departed. Sir Robert Armstrong, erstwhile Principal Private Secretary to Ted Heath and then to Harold Wilson, played very much the traditional role as Secretary to the Cabinet throughout the first administration. As with politicians, it was by no means unquestioning obedience that was sought, but rather the ability to stand up to trenchant criticism and cross-questioning and to return the fire. The higher echelons of the Thatcher administration were no place for shrinking violets; but dissenters with the capacity to fight their case did not suffer by so doing.

One break with tradition was the appointment, at the end of 1979, of Terry Burns as Chief Economic Adviser to the Chancellor. Hitherto this post had been reserved for academics with a Whitehall background (and invariably a mainstream neo-Keynesian training). Terry Burns was only 36 at the time of his appointment; he had never held a Whitehall post; and he came from the monetarist-leaning London Business School. He proved a great success. He was articulate, and got on well within the Treasury machine. But he was no doctrinaire, and not afraid to cross swords on occasion with both his immediate political masters at the Treasury and the Prime Minister. His appointment was attributable to the determination of the Financial Secretary, Nigel Lawson, although it is unlikely that this would have prevailed against Treasury resistance without the backing of the Prime Minister.

*   *   *

There is one final innovation in the machinery of government which had nothing at all to do with Prime Ministerial influence or innovation. This was a thoroughgoing reform of the system of Parliamentary Select Committees, carried through by the Leader of the House of Commons, Norman St John-Stevas. Back in the 1960s the Wilson Government had created a network of permanent Select Committees to supplement the Estimates and Public Accounts Committees, which had traditionally been responsible for seeing that public moneys went to purposes which Parliament had chosen, and that their expenditure was properly audited. These new committees had had subject remits which might or might not coincide with the roles of individual departments: Science and Technology, Nationalised Industries and Scottish Select Committees were among them. In addition the Expenditure Committee (as the Estimates Committee had been renamed) spawned a series of subject committees, on defence, social security, trade, plus a 'general committee' which concerned itself with macro-economic policy.

St John-Stevas's reforms swept most of these away, although the Public Accounts Committee was retained. Otherwise each Whitehall department was endowed with its own parliamentary watchdog. The demands on backbenchers' time were commensurately increased. So, emphatically, were the calls upon the time of ministers and senior civil servants. Whether government was thereby called the more effectively to account to the nation is a matter of conjecture. MPs on the whole believed so; so did the press – enthusiastically to begin with. But as time went by the public interest waned while the calls on ministers and their civil servants did not. One thing is certain. It was not a reform for which Mr St John-Stevas won much favour with his ministerial colleagues. As he was to discover before many months were past.

6 Rolling Back the Frontiers

Legend has it that a proximate cause of Britain's poor performance in the market place since the Second World War has been the condemnation of our industry and commerce to existence on an ideological see-saw. For five years Labour reigns, and nationalises everything that moves. Then for five years Tories rule, and sell off all that Labour has acquired. Then for five years Labour returns, and the trend is once again reversed.

Like most legends, this one has but tenuous connections with the historical record. It is true that the major portion of the steel industry was first nationalised by the postwar Labour Government, then denationalised (although not returned to any genuine competitive environment) in the 1950s, and renationalised by the first Wilson Government; and that since then successive Conservative Governments have been pledged to take it back to private enterprise (but have not, so far, done so). That is the exception. For the rest, over the 35 years from the Second World War to 1979, the pattern was a substantial extension of state ownership by each successive Labour Government, which was not reversed when the Tory Party returned to power.

The government elected in 1970 was pledged to reverse the nationalisation of steel, and to the examination of 'wider schemes for selling shares in other state concerns to the public'. In the event the only items in the state portfolio disposed of to the public by 1974 were Thomas Cook the travel agents, and a handful of pubs around Carlisle which Lloyd George had acquired in the First World War in an effort to curb drunkenness in Borders munitions factories. These paled into relative

79

insignificance when set against the nationalisation of the Rolls-Royce aeroengine business by the same administration. The 1979 election manifesto was a good deal more specific.

> We will offer to sell back to private ownership the recently nationalised aerospace and shipbuilding concerns . . . We aim to sell shares in the National Freight Corporation to the general public . . . We will also relax the Traffic Commissioner licensing regulations to enable new 'bus and other services to develop . . . the Government's temporary shareholdings [through the National Enterprise Board] to be sold off as circumstances permit . . .

The new administration did not take long to show it meant it. First to go was British Aerospace, in which a majority shareholding was floated on the stock market in 1980. This was followed by Cable & Wireless, the international communications business, in which almost half the shares were sold in 1981; Amersham International, a small specialist producer of radioactive chemicals which had hitherto been part of the nationalised atomic energy industry, sold on a wave of stock market enthusiasm in February 1982; a management 'buy-out' of the National Freight Corporation one month earlier; 51 per cent of the equity in Britoil, formed to take over the oil exploration and production interests of the British National Oil Corporation (fairly described by Nigel Lawson as 'the biggest privatisation measure ever') in November 1982; and 49 per cent of the equity in the former British Transport Docks Board in February 1983. British Rail was told to sell its hotels, its hovercraft business, the Sealink ferry service and its property portfolio; and in fact it sold almost all the hotels, got out of hovercraft, and disposed of more than £100m of property. In addition the government substantially reduced its holding in BP, and sold out from the British Sugar Corporation (the sole permitted processor of sugar beet) altogether; and powers were taken – to be exercised after the 1983 General Election – to sell a majority of shares in British Telecom (a disposal which will dwarf Britoil in size).

The injection of private capital into public businesses was only part of the story. Equally significant – in the eyes of some, even more so – was the curtailment of the privilege of monopoly. By the 1980 Transport Act, British Rail was deprived of its effective power of veto over competition from long-distance coaches; and as a result the range of choice offered to non-business travellers was transformed almost overnight, with BR obliged to try to match the private coach operators in price and service. One year later express mail and parcel services were opened up to private competition, which, again, was rapidly forthcoming; and in 1982 a rival private enterprise company called Mercury was authorised to establish its own communications network in competition with British Telecom, which was also to lose its monopoly right to install and maintain telephones in the home. Powers were also taken to authorise private firms to sell electricity of their own generation to outside customers.

Of course it was not all unimpeded progress in conformity with the government's original intentions. British Airways and British Shipbuilders, hammered by recession (and in the case of British Airways an inheritance of lacklustre management), remained stuck fast in the public sector. Yet by the end of the 1983 Parliament British Airways, under the energetic chairmanship of Sir John (now Lord) King was flexing its muscles and bidding for a place in the sales schedules for 1983 or 1984; and plans were maturing for the disposal of the profitable warship yards. Further ahead would be British Steel, where under the chairmanship of Mr Ian McGregor from 1980 onwards productivity was raised dramatically to continental (if not to Japanese) levels, and by the end of the Parliament a return to profitability was said – admittedly not for the first time – to be in sight.

British Gas presented rather a different problem. On the back of its monopoly access to North Sea gas, and the government's instruction to increase its prices dramatically for three years, the Gas Corporation remained almost embarrassingly profitable throughout the recession. There would have been no shortage of buyers had the government been minded to dispose of it in part or whole. But the government had other bits of business to see through with the Corporation first. It wanted the Corporation to get out of oil production, whether in the North Sea or in Dorset, where it had found a valuable on-shore field; and – following a highly critical report from the Monopolies Commission in 1980 – it wanted it to dispose of its retail gas showrooms.

British Gas had other ideas. Unlike some of the other nationalised industry chairmen inherited from Labour (which had tended to use the public boardrooms as depositories for worthies for whom some piece of patronage was needed), Sir Denis Rooke of British Gas was a formidable proposition. A big man with a big head and a most determined jaw who had spent his whole working life in the gas industry, he had never made any secret of his unyielding opposition to all talk of breaking up his corporation or its monopoly. And he was as good as his word. His relations with successive Energy Ministers – David Howell, and still more Nigel Lawson thereafter – were stormy at best. He not only spoke out against the plans to take away his corporation's oil interests and gas showrooms: he did not hesitate to take press advertising space to campaign against them, and to make common cause with his unions.

The government was thus obliged to issue a directive requiring him to sell the Wytch Farm in Dorset and British Gas holdings in North Sea oil. Even so, such was the tenaciousness of his rearguard action that the actual sales were still pending when the 1983 election was called. As for the showrooms, the Corporation's propaganda campaign, and the threats of strike action by the unions, scared the government backbenchers to such effect that the plans for forced disposal were pigeonholed. Sir Denis was rewarded with a second term when his first five years were up. He was, Mr Howell explained to doubting Tory colleagues, by far the best-qualified man for the job. Following the 1983 election plans were afoot to take British Gas to the market. But as an effective monopoly. Sir Denis Rooke was well content.

If gas proved difficult to move forward, coal proved impossible to save from moving backwards. In 1974 the Labour Government had published a grandiose 'Plan for Coal', according to which the retrenchment of the 1960s was to be reversed, and output raised to 150m tonnes a year by 1985, at which point the NCB would be operating without benefit of subsidy. Like the slightly earlier plans for investment in British Steel, this swiftly proved the purest moonshine. Far from improving, productivity in the coalfields had declined steadily. The annual cost of grants had trebled in the last three years of Labour rule, while the annual external financing limit had more than doubled. Nevertheless, the Tory Government on taking office made it clear that the target date for break-even in the plan for coal was to be adhered to.

But not for long. In February 1981 the Coal Board revealed its plans for pit closures needed to move to profitability. The NUM called for all-out strike action. The government, mindful of its predecessor's double drubbing by the miners, in 1972 and again in 1974, beat retreat. Extra cash was hastily found to sustain the pits in Wales and Kent, Scotland and the North which had for long served no known commercial purpose. Imports of far cheaper coal which were readily available from Australia, Poland and elsewhere were to be reduced to an 'irreducible minimum'; and the Coal Board's two key customers, the CEGB and the Steel Corporation, were promised compensation to meet the cost of leaving contracted imports safe beyond our shores.

Productivity improved as new mines were brought on stream. Unfortunately the market, apart from the CEGB, which was given little choice, shrank. Coal stocks accumulated on an heroic scale. By the end of the 1979 Parliament the National Coal Board was beginning to resemble the European dairy industry. Nevertheless the government had braved the wrath of the miners' union and its loquacious leader Arthur Scargill to nominate the redoubtable Ian McGregor for the chairmanship. It has also contrived to move coal to the power stations in case of future troubles.

So it was a chequered record. Yet neither friend nor foe could easily dispute the claim that the first Thatcher Government had done more to 'reverse the tide' of state control and monopoly than all of its postwar Tory predecessors put together. The justification for this crusade had, to ministers, several other facets apart from the need to 'roll back the frontiers of the state' on what their opponents dismissed as grounds of blinkered ideology. Privatisation (no one could find a more appealing name for it), it was pointed out, was positively to the benefit of public corporations, since it entrenched the autonomy of management. For whereas ministers could often in conformity with statute give directions to nationalised boardrooms (and the boardrooms' one redress was resignation), when a public corporation had a private shareholding the management could respond that an instruction would involve oppression of the private shareholders, and therefore were it to comply it would be in breach of its duties under the Companies Acts: a powerful defence, as experience had shown.

To the Treasury the sale of shares in public industry had numerous attractions. It reduced the amount of borrowing that would otherwise be required to bridge the gap between state spending and taxation (although if the investment institutions used cash to buy shares in a public corporation which would otherwise have been used to buy government gilt-edged issues, the Treasury's *ability* to borrow would be correspondingly diminished). Whenever 51 per cent of the equity in a public corporation was disposed of, that corporation vanished from the public sector. Since its external fund-raising no longer enjoyed government guarantee, it ceased to swell the Budget deficit (PSBR). By the same token its management was exonerated from Treasury supervision of access to capital markets.

Last, but not (desirably) least, to the general public who constituted the customers, privatisation meant that a corporation had to concern itself with market share, and hence with consumer satisfaction, in a way that the wholly state-owned business was exonerated from. And if at the same time (but only if) the privilege of monopoly was also withdrawn, the customer had somewhere else to go.

The contrary arguments were familiar enough. It was alleged that the government was giving its City friends the pickings of the state portfolio, and thereby enlarging the bills the taxpayer had to meet for what remained. It was argued that privatised corporations, and those deprived of their monopoly, would be driven to withdraw from 'public service' commitments: the railways from rural and commuter lines; the Post Office from country mail deliveries; British Telecom from call-boxes and country lines. And it was foretold that foreigners would be the primary beneficiaries: acquiring control of North Sea oil and its distribution; filling British homes with gadgetry that British Telecom and its UK suppliers could not match; undercutting British ports which were faced with the need to show a profit.

The government was not insensitive to this critique. For while it was orchestrated by those who feared the loss of bargaining power which would go with loss of monopoly and the obligation to earn a commercial return, it struck sensitive nerves on the Tory backbenches. In theory, Tory MPs were all for privatisation. In practice, a vocal minority amongst them was alarmed by talk of soaring private telephone bills, the Japanese collaring our oil and supplying all our telephones, and – worst of all, since their constituencies tended to be most at risk – vanishing branch lines and rural post deliveries.

The government responded to these anxieties in a variety of ways. In some instances – Britoil and Amersham, for example – it endowed itself with a special share which could be used to prevent control passing into foreign hands. Every effort was made to encourage small investors to buy (although they usually turned out to have taken a quick profit if one was going), and in every case employees were given the opportunity to buy shares on specially favourable terms. A brand new quango – to be called Oftel – was promised to regulate the price and supply of telephones and telephone lines following the privatisation of British Telecom and the establishment of the rival Mercury network.

7   The Storm-Clouds Gather

All things considered, the government had emerged from its first year in office with a remarkably docile party behind it at Westminster and in the country. Inflation had more than doubled; unemployment was heading for two million and above for the first time since the Great Slump of the 1930s; interest rates remained apparently stuck fast at unprecedented levels, yet monetary growth was far outside the Chancellor's chosen target range; the exchange rate was described by the Bank of England as 'excessively high', and the leaders of private industry were showing signs of despair. There *were* rebellious voices on the backbenches – former Cabinet Minister Geoffrey Rippon was calling almost every weekend for lower interest rates, and other dissenters such as Julian Critchley and Peter Tapsell did not disguise their dismay at Treasury strategy – while from the front bench Sir Ian Gilmour continued to utter veiled doubts in public, and his superior Lord Carrington unveiled doubts in private. But these seemed isolated opinions. For the most part, the rank and file may have had qualms from time to time, but put a brave face upon them. The annual Party Conference in Brighton in October 1980 was described by the *Daily Telegraph* – the house journal – as 'one of the most monotonously uncontroversial in the history of the party' (although Mr Norman St John-Stevas, Leader of the Commons, made a fierce attack on monetarist 'dogmatism' coupled with the arguments – if not the name – of Financial Secretary Nigel Lawson, while Peter Walker extolled the virtues of market management as applied to agriculture, implicitly inviting his audience to make odious comparisons with his colleagues' non-interventionist attitudes to industry). Dissent is always at a discount in the Tory Party. But the government also had two pieces of good fortune for which to be grateful. During its first two years in office there were but four by-elections, far below the average incidence from death alone. Of these four, two were in city-centre Labour rotten boroughs long overdue for extinction by the boundaries commission: in each of them the Tory candidate lost his deposit, but no one took much notice. The other two were in hitherto safe Tory seats. The first, in the North London suburbs, in December 1979, produced a respectable Tory majority. The second, in Southend in March 1980, was a close shave. Nevertheless the Tory won: and it is the spectacle of an Opposition MP marching in to take his seat for a previously bedrock Tory constituency which really scares the troops. Close shaves are soon forgotten.

The second piece of luck was predictably provided by courtesy of the Labour Party. By common consent the autumn 1980 Trades Union Congress was not a pretty sight, as the militants shouted down the moderates; but it was a vicar's tea-party by comparison with the Labour Party Conference that immediately followed. The publicity accorded to party conferences is traditionally calculated to be worth several points in the opinion polls to the performers; but in the week following the 1980 Labour Conference the party's lead slipped by 6 per cent. And then, as soon as the Tories gathered, Jim Callaghan announced his resignation as Leader of the Opposition. At other times the Tory Party managers would have regarded this as a monstrous piece of scene-stealing. In the circumstances of 1980 it was possible to view the spotlight turned on Labour's never-ending blood feuds with some quiet satisfaction.

The satisfaction was short-lived. As soon as the conferences were over the Cabinet had work to do: conclusion of the annual bargaining to decide the scale of public spending in the next financial year. It was a conclusion *pas comme les autres*.

It is one of the most hallowed of all Whitehall conventions that when Prime Minister and Chancellor are at one their will prevails. Chancellors alone are sunk: even when the Chief Secretary is a member of the Cabinet his voice tends to be discounted as the Chancellor's echo; between them they are no match for the spending departments. That is why the Treasury is doomed to discomfiture when confronted with a free-spending Premier: Harold Macmillan, for example, never made any secret of his unshakeable belief that the Treasury was hell-bent on repeating the 1930s slump, and no Chancellor of his stood a chance of controlling public spending. For the most part, however, Prime Ministers either back their Chancellors in the last ditch – Douglas-Home, Wilson, Callaghan – or, like Heath, they assume the lion's share of the task themselves. Mrs Thatcher's support for the Treasury in the 1980 public expenditure review was unstinted – indeed she tended to be in the lead. Yet they lost. It was a traumatic moment in the history of the administration.

Nor was it a particularly discreet rebuff. The Cabinet had agreed in principle before the summer holidays that an extra £2000m of savings (over and above the £1500m reduction in inherited programme spending earmarked for 1981/2 at the time of the spring Budget) must be found. Thereafter a number of key spending ministers had made helpful public noises. The Education Minister Mark Carlisle had warned his Cheshire constituents that the schools must take their share; the Welsh Secretary had pointed out that higher spending at the price of higher interest rates would eventually rebound upon the pensioners and welfare recipients as much as any others; the Secretary of State for Defence had reminded the Tory Party Conference that defence spending had to be related to what the national resources would bear.

Nevertheless, as the November deadline for actual public expenditure decisions approached, there were a number of key areas where bilateral negotiations, followed by a series of bargaining sessions presided over by the Chancellor, had been unable to close the gap between Treasury demands and departmental offers. So two long Cabinets, on 4 and 5 November, were scheduled to conclude the package. From the start things went awry for the Prime Minister and Chancellor.

Inevitably defence and social security, as the two largest and fastest-growing programmes, were at the core of the argument. Neither of the two ministers directly concerned, Francis Pym and Patrick Jenkin, were regularly numbered among the Prime Minister's Cabinet critics. Francis Pym was too cautious; while Jenkin, as already stated, was usually reckoned an economiser.

But behind Pym stood the formidable figure of his Permanent Under-Secretary, Sir Frank Cooper, determined to dig his Minister's heels in, and the Chiefs of Staff with lines out to the defence correspondents and the Tory parliamentary defence committee.

Moreover while the regular dissenters – Jim Prior, Peter Walker, Norman St John-Stevas, Ian Gilmour, and the three grandees, Carrington, Soames and Hailsham from the Lords – were not directly in the firing line, they seem to have been determined to steel the backbones of those who were.

The two biggest single economies on the Treasury agenda were £500m from defence procurement, and £600m from reductions in the uprating of benefits. Both were politically contentious. It was perhaps the Treasury's misfortune that defence came first. Francis Pym duly dug his heels in; decisions were deferred. On the morrow the Chiefs of Staff exercised their right of access to the Prime Minister. The press got wind of threats of resignation from the Defence Secretary. Finally the Treasury had to make do with an almost token £170m shaving.

Superficially the DHSS budget may have looked an easier target. The Prime Minister had frequently and publicly reaffirmed the priority attached to national defence, and the defence lobby on the backbenches tended to be drawn from her most loyal (but also vociferous) supporters. The DHSS, by contrast, was not a department for which the average Tory backbencher had much sympathy. Furthermore the Secretary of State had provisionally accepted the Treasury proposals. The Cabinet of 13 November came as all the greater shock. Patrick Jenkin read out the Prime Minister's own specific undertakings, given on television at the time of the election, to maintain the purchasing power of benefits. It was rapidly agreed that these could not be dishonoured.

In the end the Treasury emerged with just half the savings it had sought: £1060m. To make matters worse the Cabinet dissenters had seen to it that the 'victory of the wets', and the discomfiture of the Treasury, was documented almost day by day in the public prints. In the context of total spending plans exceeding £100 000m, an extra £1000m was neither here nor there. The public defiance of Treasury and Prime Minister was of altogether graver import.

Three former Prime Ministers were quick to add their individual glosses on these events. Edward Heath, invited to comment on the contemporaneous sweeping victory of the conservative Ronald Reagan in the US presidential elections, seized the opportunity to predict that the new President would learn the lesson of 'the catastrophic things' which the British saw 'happening to themselves today'. Harold Wilson reflected that his political opponents knew a thing or two about how to dispose of failed Prime Ministers. Harold Macmillan, invited to comment as he left for the United States, ostentatiously sidestepped the question to ask why Harold Wilson had himself resigned. But Ted Heath's was the intervention that mattered: not for the first time, and by no means for the last, his outspokenness was calculated to rally the backbenches behind the Prime Minister, and to embarrass and silence other critics.

The Treasury, with encouragement – indeed, propulsion – from Number 10, picked itself up off the floor and lost no time in repairing the damage. If spending could not be adequately cut then taxation would have to rise. On 24 November the Chancellor announced that from the beginning of the next financial year the cost of the employee's stamp would go up by 1 per cent to raise an extra £1000m; and that that deep-uddered milch-cow, North Sea oil, would be drained of another £1000m in petroleum revenue tax. There would also be a 1 per cent adjustment to the uprating of benefits in November 1981 to compensate for the fact that the uprating which had just taken place had been based on forecasts of inflation in the year to November 1980 which had proved over-pessimistic. With this package of additional taxes and savings under his belt Sir Geoffrey was also able to announce a cut of 2 per cent in interest rates.

The so-called Industry Act forecast, revealing the Treasury's hopes and fears for 1981, and published by convention simultaneously, made sober reading. It foresaw an annual inflation rate of 11 per cent by the end of the year ahead: worthwhile progress, but double figures for another year all the same. It held out the prospect of 'no further fall in output' in 1981 as compared with the level of the second half of 1980; but since this was down 3 per cent on the second half of 1979 (and no less than 10 per cent in respect of manufacturing industry), that was coolish comfort even if you believed it (and most commentators did not). The Government Actuary's 'assumption' for unemployment, also published at the same time, was an average of 2.7 million in 1981; and this, too, was thought by the majority of commentators to be optimistic.

Against this background, to raise additional taxation, as the Chancellor had announced was his intention, flew in the face of all postwar economic wisdom. Unless they had had the wardens of the IMF breathing down their necks, Sir Geoffrey's predecessors, without exception and regardless of party, would have been 'priming the pump' at this stage in the business cycle. 'U-turn if you want to', the Prime Minister had told her troops in Brighton, 'the lady's not for turning.' They knew now – as did her Cabinet colleagues – that she indeed meant what she said.

Yet they evidently did not believe it. As unemployment continued to soar, and factories to close through the winter, the speculation grew that, whatever the medium-term financial strategy might have said, come Budget time the Chancellor would turn the taps on. It was known that the Budget deficit for 1980/1 would far exceed Sir Geoffrey's planned figure of £8500m, largely because of the severity of the recession, and the Treasury and the Bank of England seemed to be having no difficulty in funding it. Now was the time to take another step towards fulfilment of the government's pledge to cut taxation, regardless of what had happened to public spending in the Cabinet in the autumn.

Meanwhile the balance of the Cabinet was marginally changed in the first substantial reshuffle of the administration. Shortly after the New Year, Francis Pym quit the Ministry of Defence to become Leader of the Commons. John Nott moved from the Department of Trade to Defence; John Biffen left the Treasury to replace John Nott; Leon Brittan from the Home Office was promoted Chief Secretary; and Norman St John-Stevas, having been offered, and declined, responsibility for the Arts outside the Cabinet, withdrew to the backbenches.

These moves provoked much learned exegesis. Francis Pym, it was concluded, had been paid out for his resistance to the Treasury in the preceding autumn: yet those – and there were a number – who had identified him as the likeliest beneficiary should Mrs Thatcher fall under the proverbial bus which is supposed to lie in wait for unwary Tory Premiers reckoned that he had moved to a more central position, in which he could consolidate his claim to the succession should things go badly wrong. Such speculation was to prove academic in the event. John Nott, at any rate, was readily identified: he was to be the axeman to chop the brass-hats down to the size the Treasury had in mind for them. John Biffen had somewhat disappointed the Treasury mandarins as Chief Secretary: his sceptical disposition had disinclined him to wield the axe with any relish. It was hoped that Mr Brittan, a much-admired protégé of both Geoffrey Howe and Willie Whitelaw, a former libel silk with a brilliant mind, would prove to be made of sterner stuff. As to Norman St John-Stevas, he had made the pressmen laugh at the expense of his colleagues, and not least the Prime Minister, just once too often.

This was interpreted as a stern warning to the 'wets' in Cabinet to toe the line in future. The reality was somewhat different. It was not primarily the Prime Minister whom Mr St John-Stevas had provoked. He had also been unwise enough to displease a number of his senior colleagues twice over. As Leader of the Commons it was his task to respond once a week to the ideas of backbenchers about business demanding time in the parliamentary diary. By convention they also seized the chance to comment on the topics of the day, and to invite the Leader of the House to react to their comments. Wise Leaders resist that temptation. Mr St John-Stevas did not. Foreign Office Ministers are not liable to be amused by reading the occasionally idiosyncratic opinions of the Leader of the Commons about the state of Anglo-Ruritanian relations when they are in the middle of negotiations to secure the vote of Ruritania's representative at the UN on a vital resolution.

Furthermore, St John-Stevas's new system of Select Committees had proved a heavy call on his colleagues' time and patience. Many of them had entered warnings against the new system when it had been first proposed. Mr St John-Stevas had been unimpressed: he accurately foresaw that the new Select Committees would get an excellent press and delight the backbenchers. But when his Cabinet colleagues found their worst fears fulfilled they found his witty sobriquets a little hard to bear. The St John-Stevas fan club did not reach the Cabinet table.

In terms of what had by now become the established categorisation of 'wets' and 'dries', however, there was little change. Leon Brittan, a loyal acolyte of Geoffrey Howe, had taken the place left vacant by Norman St John-Stevas. But the heavy artillery trained upon the Treasury and Number 10 was undisturbed.

To them the Chancellor's third Budget, unveiled on the eve of its parliamentary presentation in mid-March, seemed nothing less than an outrage. The CBI, in its annual valentine to the Chancellor, had called for a reduction of 2 percentage points in the national insurance surcharge paid by businesses; acceleration of the payment of regional investment grants; the maintenance of public sector capital spending programmes; no increase in direct taxation; a cut in interest rates; and 'a controlled devaluation' of the pound. Then just before the Budget the bell-wether of British industry, ICI, perpetrated the unthinkable: it cut its dividend. Somebody, somewhere, it was felt, was trying to say something to the Chancellor:

He turned a deaf ear. The Budget deficit for 1980/1 had turned out at £13 500m: almost 60 per cent above his original forecast. That was so much water under the bridge (and, according to Treasury calculations, only half of it attributable to the severity of the recession). For the year ahead the sums produced an even higher deficit – £14 000m. That, the Chancellor said, just would not do. So he proposed to cut the deficit by £3500m: £1000m to come from the increase in petroleum revenue tax foreshadowed the previous autumn; £2500m from new additions to taxation, and in particular from a decision not to adjust the tax allowances to offset the rise in prices since the 1980 Budget, while indirect tax rates were fully indexed, so that petrol went up 20p a gallon. The other proposal which attracted most attention was a once-for-all retrospective levy on the 'windfall' profits of the High Street banks resulting from the non-payment of interest on current accounts in a period of a double-figure minimum lending rate. As a result of these adjustments it was estimated that national output would be about 1 per cent lower than it would otherwise have been, and 2 per cent below the shrunken levels of 1980;

and that unemployment would rise up to and beyond three million in 1982, and stay there until the latest available date for the next election. Yet with all this, after a year in which the 'volume' of public spending had risen by almost 2 per cent instead of falling, as the Chancellor had intended, by 0.7 per cent, a further rise was now projected for the year ahead. Moreover the modesty of that rise depended on the expectation – based on hope rather than any past experience – that costs, and particularly pay, would grow more slowly in the public services than in the private sector.

Presented with this brimstone draught, a number of the Cabinet dissenters let it be known that they had toyed with resignation. In the end, like others in similar circumstances before them, they decided to 'stay and fight for their beliefs', while informing sympathetic journalists that never again would they allow the Treasury to confront them with a *fait accompli*. One unbridled backbench critic, Mr Peter Tapsell, who was known to share the amazement of his admirers that his services had never been called for in Great George Street, announced that 'Sir Geoffrey Howe has now lost the confidence of broad sections of the City, of industry, of the Cabinet and of the Conservative Parliamentary Party. The Prime Minister . . . owes it to the country and to the Conservative Party to find a Chancellor . . . who will command confidence and offer hope.' But Sir Geoffrey's Cabinet colleagues knew that the Prime Minister was right up there beside him. As if to underline the point, speaking to a gathering of businessmen a few days after the Budget, she complained bitterly that 'those who are most critical of extra taxes are those who are most vociferous in demanding extra spending . . . having demanded extra spending they are not prepared to face the consequences of their own actions . . .' There was a widespread feeling that her remarks were directed to targets closer to 10 Downing Street than the businessmen to whom they happened to be addressed.

Nevertheless it would have been hard to dispute Mr Tapsell's general assessment of the reception accorded to the 1981 Budget, even though his count of voices around him on the Tory backbenches smacked of wishful thinking. Within ten days Sir Geoffrey's judgement had been roundly challenged by the Commons Treasury Committee, and before March was out it was the subject of a broadside from no less than 364 academic economists in the pages of *The Times*. The Chief Secretary, Leon Brittan, insisted that recovery from the recession was inevitable, as night followed day. He found few takers. Anatole Kaletsky, in the pages of the *Financial Times*, noted:

> It is now more or less common ground in the financial world and among politicians of all parties that the monetarist cure for inflation has failed. Nobody, even in the Conservative Party, or at the London Business School, seems seriously to believe that inflation will fall substantially below the rate of 8 percent which the Government inherited in 1979. The gilt-edged market is signalling its conviction that from now on the trend in the inflation rate will be rising.

The government could ride out the storm of criticism from the academic establishment, the desperation increasingly voiced by the captains of industry, and the grumbles of the dissenters within the Cabinet so long as the Conservative Parliamentary Party held behind it; and for the most part it continued to do so. But the political ground was shifting dramatically. Following the victory of the left-wing candidate, Mr Michael Foot, in Labour's leadership contest in November 1980, and the subsequent decision to give the dominant voice in future contests to the union block votes, the break-up of the Labour Party, so long predicted prematurely, had at last begun. Two former senior Labour Ministers and MPs, Dr Owen and Mr Bill Rodgers, together with the former Chancellor and President of the EEC Commission, Mr Roy Jenkins, and Mrs Williams, who had lost her seat in 1979, had launched the SDP in January, and in due course they were joined by nine other defectors from the Labour ranks. Up to a score of others were known to be hovering on the brink of joining them.

In theory Labour's public disarray should have been good news for the government. In practice the emergence of the SDP constituted an ominous threat. Tory Governments in trouble had traditionally suffered defections at the grassroots not to Labour, but to the Liberals. The Liberals, however, while they had often scored dramatic victories at the Tories' expense in mid-term by-elections, lacked any practical experience in government and had usually failed to hold the majority of their by-election converts when the ensuing General Election arrived. The SDP, by contrast, was well endowed with ministerial talent; and moving, as it was bound to do, into close alliance with the Liberals, seemed to pose a major threat. If the opinion polls were any guide, the two parties taken together had swept into a commanding lead in popular support over both the government and the Labour Opposition within months of the SDP breakaway.

Then, one week after the Budget, the Tory MP for North-west Norfolk, Christopher Brocklebank-Fowler, suddenly announced his defection to the SDP. Brocklebank-Fowler, a relatively rare Tory backbench enthusiast for the Third World, was hardly any sort of bell-wether, and it was known that he had been at odds with his local constituency association to such an extent that his readoption was thought to be in doubt. Nevertheless such a rare apostasy sent shivers down the spines of government business managers. It was widely reported that at least three other backbenchers on what was usually described as the left of the Tory Party were 'considering their future'. With the political commentators almost wholly absorbed by what was seen as the struggle for the soul of the Tory Party between the 'wets' and 'dries' (as the two contending viewpoints were now universally known), the Chairman of the Party, Lord Thorneycroft, himself publicly confessed to 'rising damp'.

He remained, however, remarkably fortunate in not having to rally the troops in the country for a crop of by-elections. The summer produced but one, in the safe Labour seat of Warrington. Mrs Shirley Williams, regarded at the time as the most charismatic of the SDP leaders, agonised about taking up the challenge, and thought better of it. But Mr Jenkins did not shrink; and his courage was very nearly rewarded. The Tory vote collapsed and a somewhat oddly-chosen candidate lost his deposit. Mr Jenkins came within 2000 votes of unseating Labour. The blow was heaviest to Labour: nevertheless there was no gainsaying the evidence that the SDP had caught the popular imagination – or at least that of the media.

It was hardly to be wondered at, therefore, that the usual long hours of the midsummer debates upon the Finance Bill to carry Sir Geoffrey's third Budget into law produced a crop of trouble for the government business managers. A number of Tory backbenchers with City connections took vocal exception to the retrospective profits levy on the banks; and one of them, Tim Renton, having announced his intention to vote against that proposition, was required to resign his position as Parliamentary Private Secretary to John Biffen, President of the Board of Trade.

The bank levy, however, was not a proposal which the Labour Opposition could conceivably oppose; so the government was in no danger. Far more serious was the rebellion on the backbenches against the increase in taxation on petrol. Petrol and derv taxation was always liable to be a sensitive subject on the Tory backbenches, where the numerous MPs from widely-scattered rural constituencies, particularly in the Celtic fringes, complained that the inadequacies of country transport made motoring a necessity of life. Eventually the Chancellor was warned by the government whips that unless he yielded on the derv tax increase he would face defeat, since the Opposition Parties had predictably hustled in behind the Tory rebels. On 30 April he bowed to the inevitable, recommending acceptance of a backbench amendment to cut the increase in the tax on derv from 20p to 10p. The amount of revenue thereby forgone – some £130m in a full year – was hardly material in terms of a forecast deficit of more than £9000m. It was characteristic of the mood of grim determination which now gripped the Treasury that Sir Geoffrey should have promptly announced that he would recoup the lost revenue in other ways. And this he did, announcing at the beginning of July that the duty on a packet of cigarettes, increased by 14p in the Budget, would be raised another 3p. It was a judicious choice, since many of the natural critics of Treasury strategy were also vociferous opponents of smoking. Nevertheless what was widely interpreted as Sir Geoffrey's 'vindictiveness' against successful dissent deepened the mood of resistance in the Cabinet.

Perhaps the moment of greatest peril in the lifetime of the first Thatcher administration occurred at this point when three inner-city areas, Toxteth in Liverpool, Brixton in South London and Moss Side in Manchester, each with large West

Indian populations, erupted in communal violence. There had been outbreaks of trouble between the black communities and the police before – notably in Bristol. But the scale of the violence on this occasion was unprecedented: in Toxteth for a period of hours the rioters effectively took over. The most obvious common thread linking the three centres of violence was the size of the immigrant community; and while unemployment was very high in Toxteth, in Brixton it was below the national average, and far below the levels in some other equally downtrodden inner-city areas such as Glasgow where no trouble occurred. Nevertheless the riots were seized upon by the government's critics, and dissenters in the Cabinet, as evidence that the 'monetarist experiment', and the unemployment attributed to it, were putting the social fabric of the nation under strains it could not take. For once the Prime Minister's nerve seemed momentarily to falter: it seems conceivable that had the critics round the Cabinet table mounted a united campaign for a change of course, their demands might at this moment have prevailed.

But they never did. Truth to tell, while they shared a common sense of deep foreboding about the destination of the course the government was following, they were by no means of one voice about the direction that it *ought* to take. Only Sir Ian Gilmour – and perhaps Peter Walker – favoured wholesale, old-fashioned 'reflation'. Jim Prior, the only prominent dissenter with a mainline economic department behind him, favoured reconciliation and a new concordat with the unions: but he did not share Gilmour's expansionism, not least, perhaps, because he foresaw the inflationary pressures which such a change of gear would generate, and unlike Gilmour had no appetite for another attempt at legalised control of wage bargaining. Lord Carrington, rather like Sir Keith Joseph at the corresponding phase of the Heath Government, preferred to keep his head down behind his departmental brief. Francis Pym was widely seen as the potential beneficiary of a palace revolution, but he was not the man to set the wheels in motion. Lord Soames, bruised and frustrated in the long dispute with the civil service in the spring and early summer, was increasingly disaffected but somewhat at a distance from the central economic argument.

At any rate the moment of uncertainty soon passed. A Committee of Enquiry under Lord Scarman was set up to investigate the causes of the riots; Michael Heseltine was given a special remit to raise morale on Merseyside; and before the Commons rose for the summer recess the Prime Minister announced the commitment of an extra £150m in the current financial year on urban aid and youth employment programmes. But when the Cabinet met for its annual late-summer review of spending plans for the following year, what was billed by most of the political and economic commentators as a head-on collision between the 'wets' and the 'dries" notably failed to materialise. Admittedly the Treasury's attempt to get spending departments to agree in principle to a cut of either 5 or 3 per cent in all programmes to bring expenditure back on course and to leave room for tax cuts in the 1982 Budget found few takers, and all was left to play for in the autumn round of bilateral negotiations between the Chief Secretary and the departmental ministers. But a few weeks later the Treasury successfully and – given the range of support mustered behind it – surprisingly managed to abort a grandiose plan to build a North Sea gas-gathering pipeline with state finance at a cost optimistically put at £2700m.

The Royal Wedding at the end of July, on a day of glorious summer weather after weeks of rain and cold, gave an immense boost to national morale. Nevertheless the clouds which overhung the government's horizon as the summer holidays began were ominous indeed. Unemployment was about to break through the three million barrier for the first time since the early 1930s. The Chancellor and Chief Secretary insisted that the recession had 'bottomed out': there was as yet little to show for it, and the Treasury's summer forecasts were reported to show a scaled-down recovery – 1 per cent growth – in 1982. Inflation had dropped to 11 per cent for the first time since the General Election, but was soon expected to accelerate again. Because of the absence of collated statistics and delays in tax collection due to the civil service strike nobody knew for sure what was happening to the monetary aggregates; but in the first quarter of the financial year the government had had to borrow two-thirds of what it planned to borrow through to April 1982. On top of all this, the pound had been plummeting as American interest rates soared to 20 per cent. The Bank of England was reported to be intervening heavily to hold the exchange rate; but it was generally held to be only a matter of time before London money rates would have to be allowed to move up in sympathy with New York if sterling's weakness was not to reverse the progress so painfully made in the battle with domestic inflation. To rub salt in the wounds, an eminent Swiss economist, Professor Hans Niehans, whom the Prime Minister had consulted during her brief summer holiday the year before, and who was billed as one of her staunchest admirers, published an assessment of British economic management which concluded that monetary policy had been ruinously tight, and carried much of the responsibility for the severity of the recession: thus echoing precisely the charges that were weekly levelled by the Opposition and the academic establishment in Britain. According to the opinion polls the government was now trailing both Labour and the new Alliance of Liberals and Social Democrats in popular esteem; and Mrs Thatcher was deemed to win the contest for the title of 'the worst Prime Minister in living memory' in a canter (trailed by Neville Chamberlain 48 to 15).

She was evidently unimpressed. As ministers began to trickle back to desks towards the end of August, increasingly circumstantial rumours circulated that the Prime Minister was to make a major government reshuffle. At the centre of the speculation was the position of Jim Prior. The Prime Minister, it was said, intended him to go to Northern Ireland. He, it was further said, was not minded to go. Indeed the press reported in a degree of detail which seemed only compatible with extensive briefing by the interested parties that he would, if asked to go to Northern Ireland, decline the invitation and defy the Prime Minister to send him to the backbenches as an open focus of revolt. The challenge to the Prime Minister's authority was unprecedented in the history of Tory Governments in modern times.

The reshuffle eventually occurred in mid-September, and it proved indeed to be the most far-reaching since the government was formed. Sir Keith Joseph, who had appeared for many months to find the interventionist instincts of the Department of Industry painfully hard to reconcile with his own philosophical distaste for intervention, moved to the somewhat less exposed position of Secretary of State for Education, displacing Mark Carlisle who withdrew without pleasure but without recrimination to the backbenches. David Howell, who was known to have found himself no match for the Prime Minister's sometimes abrasive style of Cabinet management, was shifted sideways to the Ministry of Transport. At Energy his place was taken by Nigel Lawson, arguably the dominant personality at the Treasury, who had been bitterly disappointed to have Leon Brittan parachuted in on top of him as Chief Secretary in the spring. He now won his reward with elevation to the Cabinet. Patrick Jenkin moved from the Department of Health and Social Security to the Department of Industry, his place being taken by Norman Fowler from Transport.

To this extent, the changes did not have a particularly 'ideological' imprint (although the elevation of Nigel Lawson brought in an eloquent ally of the Prime Minister). The other changes were a good deal more dramatic. Lord Soames, whose handling of the civil service dispute had notably irritated the Prime Minister, was dismissed and responded with an icy resignation letter. Sir Ian Gilmour was also dismissed and responded with a public comment that the government was heading for the rocks. Lord Thorneycroft, the Party Chairman, whose publicly-expressed doubts about Treasury Ministers' claims regarding the end of the recession had irritated the Prime Minister in the summer, and whose approach to the management of Central Office had begun to create controversy, gave way to a suave and popular junior minister from the Department of Trade, Cecil Parkinson.

But the cleanest sweep was reserved for the Department of Employment. Jim Prior was indeed consigned to Northern Ireland, a position which he accepted after hours of agonising and with the modest face-saver of retention of his place on the central 'E', or Economic, Committee of the Cabinet. Of his two most loyal acolytes one, Nicholas Scott, went with him to Northern Ireland, while the other, Jim Lester, retired to the backbenches. Jim Prior's place was taken by Norman Tebbit, Minister of State at the Department of Industry, who was regarded by the 'wet' wing of the Tory Party as the unacceptable face of Thatcherite Toryism. The *coup de grâce*, in the eyes of the Prime Minister's critics and opponents in the government and press, was the appointment of Nicholas Ridley from the Foreign Office and the present author to make up the Treasury team.

It was indeed a sea-change. For the first time since she had come to office the Prime Minister had built herself a clear majority in the Cabinet. A vociferous critic in Sir Ian Gilmour had finally been put beyond the tent; and the Department of Employment, where a single junior minister, Peter Morrison, had hitherto carried the Prime Minister's standard, had been purged and brought within the fold. Most striking of all, Jim Prior had been caught out bluffing publicly, and his bluff had publicly been called. His credibility had inevitably taken quite a buffeting.

The circumstances of Jim Prior's embarrassment were not quite as they seemed. When originally approached about a move to Northern Ireland he had not been averse. Throughout his tenure of the Department of Employment he had been at loggerheads with the Prime Minister, since his distaste for trades union legislation conflicted with her enthusiasm. And whereas the Prime Minister's views coincided with the views of party activists and industrial supporters, those of Jim Prior did not. Northern Ireland offered the prospect of, if not a less contentious atmosphere – Northern Ireland would never be that – at least a change of air. So he agreed. Then he learnt the name of his chosen successor. At this, vigorously encouraged by his entourage, he struck. But it was too late.

That was as it might be. For the moment what counted was that the Prime Minister had reasserted her authority in the most dramatic manner possible, and one of her more important known adversaries had bowed the knee.

That did not mean that dissent within the party was cowed and silenced. On the contrary the Party Conference in Blackpool that September was perhaps the most turbulent since the celebrated occasion 18 years earlier when it had been thrown directly into a leadership election. The conference managers performed their usual magic, and even the dreaded ritual moment when Ted Heath had to encounter his successor before the television cameras passed off with adequate decorum. The former leader got a rough reception for his dismissive analysis of government management of the economy, and in general the loyalty of the grassroots was unshaken. But the commentators did not waste their time in the conference hall. They did the rounds of the fringe meetings, where evicted former ministers such as Norman St John-Stevas and Ian Gilmour made Treasury 'rigidity' their target; while those who had stayed behind such as Peter Walker and Michael Heseltine used opacity to let their messages of disagreement filter through. Even more appetising were the comments passed by dissenters in the *couloirs*: Lord Carrington staked out his attitude by asking any Treasury Minister he met what damage they had inflicted on the economy in the previous 24 hours. Most appetising of all was the announcement that Geoffrey Rippon, a Cabinet Minister in the Heath administration who had not enjoyed preferment under Mrs Thatcher, was prepared to let his name go forward as a challenger for the leadership of the party when the House of Commons resumed at the end of October. It was not at all a credible challenge: Rippon did not have a backbench following or coterie, and plainly invited a crushing rebuff. But he was widely seen as a seat-warmer for a more formidable challenger – Mr Edward du Cann?, even Mr Heath himself? – who might emerge if the groundswell of revolt gained momentum. It would have been hard to find a journalist at Blackpool willing to take bets on a Tory victory in the next election; but easy to find those prepared to speculate on alternative names to lead the party into it. Majority opinion among the commentators was that the party was heading for a defeat of 1945 proportions, or worse. The party faithful whistled to keep their spirits up, or sought consolation round the bars.

8 The Tide Turns

Autumn 1981 marked the halfway stage of the natural span of the Parliament elected in May 1979. It also turned out to mark the low-water mark in the government's fortunes. Brave hearts were needed to see it that way at the time. An administration which had set out to release the national spirit of enterprise by cutting public spending and taxation had so far achieved a substantial rise in both. Inflation had been pulled back to where it started, but was now forecast to rise again. The private sector appeared to be flat on its back. The flow of funds to public corporations continued on a massive scale. Monetary policy, presented as the cornerstone of the government's counter-inflation strategy, was threatening to escape control yet again. Interest rates across the world were rising steeply, promising to set off a secondary recession on top of the one of unprecedented postwar severity which had already occurred. Unemployment had passed the three million mark, and showed little sign of abating. According to the opinion polls, popular support for the government in general, and the Prime Minister in particular, was lower than hitherto recorded since the statistics had been first compiled. Notwithstanding the autumn reshuffle, relations within the Cabinet were exceptionally acrimonious: even men like John Biffen, who were usually ranked among the Prime Minister's loyalists, had begun to voice distaste for her manner of conducting Cabinet debate. The Treasury's attempts to bring public spending for 1982/3 back in line with the totals forecast in the spring Budget had once more largely failed, leaving an expected slippage of some £3½bn.

Then, as the Chancellor departed for the annual meetings of the International Monetary Fund and the World Bank in Washington, the London financial markets began to show signs of moderate panic. The pound was tumbling, notwithstanding reportedly substantial intervention by the Bank of England, and the sale of gilts – essential to mop up excessive growth in the monetary aggregates – had come to a grinding halt. Back in August, after months of discussion between the Bank of England, the Treasury and Professor Alan Walters from 10 Downing Street, the Bank had announced the abandonment of its minimum lending rate (the system by which, since the abolition of the old bank rate, it had indicated to the markets what it wanted to happen to short-term interest rates). In future a somewhat arcane formula was to prevail, by which interest rates would – at least in theory – be chosen primarily by the financial markets themselves, although the Bank reserved the right to apply an overdrive. Now, after urgent transatlantic phone calls, it was agreed that the Bank should use its overdrive to lift the base rates of the commercial banks by 1 per cent. The markets were unassuaged, and in October a second rise was deemed unavoidable. The sale of gilts resumed; the pound was stabilised; but the CBI and independent commentators feared that such recovery as might be materialising would be swiftly knocked upon the head.

Hardly surprisingly, the Tory Party in the country was taking a battering. In October the Liberals, fielding a candidate who failed to impress the commentators or anybody else, turned a 4000 Conservative General Election majority over Labour in Croydon Northwest into a 3000 Liberal lead. In November Mrs Shirley Williams achieved a much more dramatic breakthrough for the SDP. In Crosby, a middle-class suburb of Liverpool, she overturned a Tory majority of 19 000. The Liberals and the SDP were earnestly discussing the distribution of portfolios between them after the next election: and the press was half-inclined to take the discussion seriously.

Yet beneath it all the government was less vulnerable than it looked. The rebellious talk of Blackpool had swiftly petered out when MPs got back to Westminster. Nothing more was heard of the Geoffrey Rippon challenge. The majority of Tory backbenchers probably shared the opinion of the political correspondents that most of them were doomed (according to one extrapolation of the Crosby by-election result, the Tories could expect to win a single seat if that voting pattern were repeated when the election came). But far from inclining them to revolt the prospect rather made them beat their chests to try to keep their spirits up. The 'wets', for the most part, withdrew sulking to their tents. It was too late now, with more than half the life-span of the Parliament behind them, to secure a change of course which would produce results in time to divert the voters.

And, albeit doubted and derided, there were some chinks of dawn in eastern windows. The CBI's monthly and quarterly surveys of member firms' expectations had stopped descending further into depths of gloom from the late summer on. Unemployment, though still rising, was no longer rising quite so steeply. The steep fall in the exchange rate, whatever it might presage for inflation expectations, responded to the pleas of industry. From December onwards the opinion polls too began to tell a notably more cheerful story for both government and Prime Minister. By the early spring the three national political groups were running neck and neck; and while Roy Jenkins seized the Tories' last remaining seat in Glasgow in March, there was nothing approaching the landslide swing to the Alliance seen at Crosby.

Then came Falklands.

Already there is quite a library of books about the Falklands War, and this is not the place – or the author – to add to it. But obviously no survey of the first four Thatcher years can be compiled without consideration of the impact of the war on the course of the administration and its performance.

The Franks Commission of senior Privy Counsellors appointed in the aftermath of the recovery of the Falkland Islands from Argentine domination to examine and report on how the incident occurred concluded, like the magistrate in the case of Albert and the lion at Blackpool zoo, 'that no one was rightly to blame'. This was widely regarded as an eccentric verdict; the Labour Party, which had been hoping to make political capital out of the mistakes it believed the review was bound to reveal, was particularly distressed that its own representative on the Commission should have gone along with such a tame conclusion. Yet it is by no means clear how the Commission as a whole could have come to any other, for if there is one thing that emerges with clarity from the report it is the failure of communications, not so much within the government itself, as between the government and public opinion in the country at large. Nor is it easy to see, in all the circumstances, how that could have been avoided. In days gone by, when national newspapers maintained a network of resident correspondents around the globe, some awareness of the degree of Argentine national commitment to 'recovery' of sovereignty over the islands might have been brought home to the British public. The cost of such a network, and the resultant reliance upon 'visiting firemen' despatched from London only when trouble flared, meant that British newspaper readers for the most part basked in blissful ignorance of Argentinian sentiment.

As a result, whenever, from the later 1960s onwards, successive British Governments sought to enter into negotiations with a view to disposing of this long-standing bone of contention between the two countries, the public reaction in Britain, faithfully reflected in Parliament, was that the Foreign Office was hell bent on getting shot of a relatively painless responsibility in defiance of the known wishes of a small group of loyal settlers of undoubted British stock, and thereby subjecting them to alien domination by an odious and despotic military government in Buenos Aires.

The Foreign Office, of course, was well aware of the strength of Argentinian feelings, and the probability that they would eventually lead to some form of military intervention unless they were assuaged. From time to time – most notably, as the Franks Report revealed, following the visit of Foreign Office Minister Nicholas Ridley to Buenos Aires and the Falklands at the end of 1980 – it did seek to explain to Fleet Street editors the dimensions of the problem and the reasons for trying to find a compromise solution. But it is easy to understand that an orchestrated campaign to arouse public opinion at home to the risk of potential conflict would have been seen at any given moment as liable to encourage the Argentinians to turn the risk into reality.

Yet public ignorance had a double consequence. Not only did it lead to suspicion of the motives of the Foreign Office in seeking a negotiated settlement: it also meant that there was no groundswell of support for the only logical alternative, which was the maintenance of a sufficiently powerful defensive screen in the South Atlantic to protect the islands.

In retrospect it may seem obvious that the solution canvassed by the Foreign Office under the Callaghan administration in the late 1970s, and again in late 1980, by which formal sovereignty over the islands would have been surrendered to the Argentinians in return for effective continuity of UK administration, would have been the best way out. Unfortunately, for it to have secured parliamentary endorsement acceptance by the islanders was essential; and for that acceptance to be forthcoming the islanders had to be persuaded that continuation of the *status quo* was not a viable alternative. They were unlikely to be so persuaded so long as Parliament reacted with hostility to all talk of change.

The Foreign Office evidently hoped that the Argentinians would come to the rescue by cutting communications with the mainland on which the islanders relied, thereby convincing them that things could not continue as they were. The Argentinians did not oblige. So all three parties continued on collision course. It may be – as was alleged at the time and subsequently – that the decision to withdraw HMS *Endurance* from the South Atlantic in the summer of 1981 convinced the Argentinians that if they struck the British would go quietly. But they could have felt they had that signal at any time. For as one British diplomat was quoted as saying, the British had sought to make it clear for years that they would welcome seduction, and only drew the line at rape: and that is a message that invites misunderstanding between nations just as much as between individuals.

Besides, from the Argentinian standpoint it was not just the announcement of the planned withdrawal of the *Endurance* coming on top of all the other signs of British reluctance to try conclusions which made it reasonable to expect that London would bow to a *fait accompli*. The precedents suggested that action to terminate the survival of one of the remaining outposts of old empire would be greeted with averted gaze by the international community. As Jo Grimond pointed out, when the Indians had seized Goa by brute force and in defiance of the wishes of a Catholic population who were just as loyal to

Portugal as the Falklanders were to Britain, no one lifted a finger. Had Argentina been ruled by Castro look-alikes instead of by a bunch of right-wing military, the world response would surely have been different – and perhaps the response from London too. Certainly it was the 'fascist' nature of the regime responsible for the invasion which seemed to weigh more heavily with most Opposition MPs, and even some Tory ones as well, than the fact of the invasion.

Among Tories at Westminster, however, when the news of the invasion was confirmed late on the afternoon of Friday, 2 April, the target in the firing-line was not General Galtieri so much as the government front bench. Having rubbished every attempt to resolve the controversy by compromise, the Tory backbench foreign affairs and defence buffs were outraged by the consequences. Many of them subscribed instinctively to the proposition that the Foreign Office was 'not on our side', and had some scores to settle for what they regarded as the betrayal of White Rhodesia. They were also deeply suspicious of John Nott, who was seen as a Treasury axeman hellbent on undermining the nation's defence, and in particular its sea-power.

So when the House of Commons met in special session on Saturday 3 April it was in a very ugly mood. Two Tory backbenchers, both ex-Foreign Office diplomats, who dared to call for a negotiated solution, were howled down by their colleagues; and John Nott, who unwisely tried to divert his followers by questioning claims from Jim Callaghan, David Owen and others on the Opposition benches that the previous Labour Government had successfully warded off the threat of Argentinian invasion of the islands in 1978, suffered even worse. Had the Prime Minister not announced the immediate despatch of a task force it does not seem fanciful to speculate that the government might have fallen that weekend.

As it was, John Nott and Lord Carrington faced a bitter and ruthless grilling from a heavily-attended meeting of backbench Tory MPs that afternoon. Although John Nott's performance in the debate was universally condemned and his days in office were thought to be numbered, it was the role of the Foreign Office which bore the brunt of criticism at the upstairs party meeting. There seems little doubt that it was the tone of this meeting which determined Lord Carrington to resign. The Foreign Secretary had never served in the House of Commons, and his admiration for the party grassroots and backbenchers had always stopped a long way short of rapture. The hostility displayed on this occasion towards his department and all its works served as final confirmation of his opinion of what had been happening to the party. It was not a club he found sympathetic, or even bearable. All the Prime Minister's genuine and heartfelt efforts to persuade him to stay on proved unavailing.

So Lord Carrington departed with the task force. The latter was embarked on a most hazardous undertaking. Comparisons were inevitably made with Suez. They were apt in but one respect: this was that on both occasions the official Opposition stood shoulder to shoulder with the government and its backbenchers in expressions of initial outrage and calls for whatever action might be needed to recover British rights and property; and that on both occasions this solidarity proved remarkably short-lived. In every other respect the two dramas differed. Colonel Nasser had seized a commercial asset on Egyptian soil, not a disputed territory across hundreds of miles of sea. The initial response to Suez had been the search for a negotiated solution, with military intervention held in putative reserve. But above all the international environment was totally different. At Suez it had been the French, and not the British Government, who had been in the lead (and had they been allowed to proceed with their initial plan to supply Israel with air cover while the Israelis dealt with Egypt, it might well have worked). Colonel Nasser was already a hero to the Arab world, and solidly supported by every Arab government; while the US administration was from the start disinclined to see President Eisenhower's campaign for reelection disrupted by trouble in the Middle East. Argentina, by contrast, was effectively isolated. Other South American states for the most part expressed support: but with no enthusiasm. The United States was certainly concerned about the possible repercussions of the Falklands War on its relations with Latin America, and feared lest Argentina should be driven to turn to the Soviet Union. But when forced to choose, President Reagan unhesitatingly chose Britain. So did the large majority of our Community partners – albeit less unhesitatingly. Most other governments were reluctant to be seen in close consort with such unfashionable allies as the Buenos Aires generals.

A closer – but even more ominous – parallel might have been drawn with the Russo-Japanese War of 1904–5. For the British, like the Russians, had to send a task force halfway round the world to retake a territory almost on the opponents' doorstep. And the Russians, having travelled from the Baltic to the Pacific, on arrival at their destination had been promptly sunk. The Tsarist regime survived Port Arthur (although it arguably suffered a wound from which it never recovered): it is hard to believe that the Thatcher Government would have survived a similar calamity. Yet while there was good reason to expect that if battle were once joined on land the Argentinian conscripts would prove no match for the highly-trained British professionals, the task force on the high seas, far beyond the range of land-based air cover, was bound to be vulnerable to the sophisticated modern armoury the Buenos Aires junta had assembled over the years. There was no doubting the enthusiastic popular support in Britain for the launching of the task force; whether that enthusiasm would have survived a heavy loss of British lives on the high seas is a very different matter.

There was a lesser hazard. As the task force sailed across the Atlantic to its destination, the search for a negotiated settlement continued at a frantic pace in Washington, New York and London. Since the United Nations had formally endorsed the need for the Argentinian army of occupation to be withdrawn from the islands, and since this would have been a peculiarly bitter pill for the generals to swallow, the chances of a sucessful outcome were never high. Nevertheless if against the odds an internationally acceptable compromise had been arrived at it would presumably have had to involve some substantial dilution – even abandonment – of UK sovereignty over the islands. That would not have gone down well on the government backbenches.

In the event, of course, all such fears turned out liars. The operation was a copy-book example of its kind, achieving all its objectives with minimal loss of British life. The national morale was given a palpable lift. After 35 years of almost uninterrupted postwar retreat and shrinkage, highlighted by such signal humiliations as Suez, the majority of the electorate was reconciled to the assumption that we lacked both the means and the nerve to mount an independent military operation of this kind. The discovery that we had both after all was all the sweeter. In the Prime Minister's phrase, 'Britain walked tall.' That was not an overstatement.

Her own reputation and authority, inevitably, were massively enhanced. She could not have failed to know that for her personally the stakes were desperately high; but although there were occasions – notably the night the news was brought of the sinking of HMS *Sheffield* by an Argentine missile – when she was visibly both tired and shaken, in the view of those who watched her conduct of the war from close at hand her nerve and resolution never faltered. Following the capture of Port Stanley and the surrender of the Argentinian forces it was Enoch Powell who characteristically summed up the national reaction. Recalling how, on that traumatic Saturday when the Commons debated the invasion, he had predicted that the 'Iron Lady's' metal was to be put to the test, he told her that it had indeed been tested: and found true.

The so-called 'Falklands factor' faded fairly swiftly over the final year of the 1979 Parliament as the excitement of the campaign receded into history. There was something else, however, that was not so swift to fade. Throughout her time at 10 Downing Street Mrs Thatcher had consistently emphasised her determination not to be diverted from her chosen strategies: 'There is no alternative', and 'The lady's not for turning' had become her – frequently derided – catch phrases. The Falklands War was widely seen as the most dramatic confirmation possible of that steely resolve. Even her bitterest opponents began to display a grudging – almost horrified – respect. In the country at large those who had lost their jobs and seen their businesses collapse in bankruptcy were liable to comment 'well, she may have bust us, but by God she's got guts'. It was not a sentiment expressed about her predecessors since the middle 1950s.

As already mentioned, the opinion polls had suggested a slow revival in support for both Prime Minister and government from the previous midwinter onwards. As the Falklands

War progressed this revival gathered momentum. The local government elections in May proved something of a minor landslide, and on the doorstep the Falklands inevitably took precedence over rates and refuse collection. At a by-election in the safe Tory seat of Beaconsfield at the end of May the Tory candidate was returned with precisely the same proportion of the votes as his predecessor had collected in 1979; and in June, when the brave decision of one of the Labour defectors to the SDP to submit his new allegiance to the verdict of his electors in a by-election in a south London suburb, the government actually won a seat for the first time in a generation.

Back at Blackpool in the previous autumn one of the most experienced of the lobby correspondents had told the author that nothing could save the government from annihilation at the next election. Now a heartfelt complaint that ministerial office meant half-pay for a doubled workload brought an unfeeling response from the same correspondent. 'Well, you'd better get used to it, for you're stuck with it for the next Parliament as well unless she sacks you.' Needless to say he was wrong again. But his changing predictions certainly reflected a popular consensus: a second term for Mrs Thatcher was now seen as almost as ineluctable as nine months earlier it had been unthinkable. Fortune is indeed a fickle jade.

9 Easing the Brake

While the generals on the other side of the world were preparing their *coup de foudre* the Treasury, as is its custom when the minds of less high-thinking citizens have turned to winter sports, was considering what to put in Sir Geoffrey Howe's fourth Budget. Some things were looking a good deal more propitious. After the precipitous rise in US interest rates in the late summer of 1981, and the subsequent two-fold upwards adjustment to London rates, the cost of money was beginning to ease once more. Contrary to most predictions (including the Treasury's own) inflation had only risen by 1 per cent to 12 per cent in the autumn, and was soon expected to resume its descent; and 1981 had produced an all-time record current account payments surplus of £6000m. This had no doubt reflected the severity of the recession; but exports of manufactures had held up in the face of all the warnings by manufacturers of imminent withdrawal from their foreign markets. Government borrowing was forecast to be almost spot on the Budget-time forecast of £10½bn.

There were some debit items in the balance sheet. Judging by the latest soundings conducted by the CBI the autumn rise in interest rates had applied a touch of frost to the first buds of recovery; and this message was confirmed by the Treasury's own soothsayers. There was seen to be a real risk of a 'W'-shaped recession, with a second – albeit much shallower – downturn following the tentative and marginal progress of the second half of 1981. Yet all the broader measures of the money stock were running well above the upper end of the range chosen for £M3 in March 1981; and a sharp increase in public spending programmes was in prospect following the successful resistance mounted by departments in the autumn.

Much learned exegesis took place in the winter of 1981/2 regarding the meaning of the performance of the monetary

115

aggregates. In 1980 this had been distorted – to an extent which could only be guessed at – by the removal of the 'corset'; in the early months of 1981 it had been similarly distorted by the civil service strike which had both disrupted the collation of the figures and (by forcing the postponement of tax collection) changed the underlying data. But by the end of 1981 the extraneous influences were fading fast: yet still the chosen target aggregate – £M3 – was proving remarkably elusive.

Critics, naturally, enjoyed the Treasury's apparent uncertainty. Edward Heath had begun to make a point of congratulating the Chancellor on abandonment of 'monetarist dogmatism'. Sir Ian Gilmour, with more elegance than meaning, dismissed the whole debate as 'the uncontrollable in pursuit of the indefinable' (or vice versa, as Oscar Wilde might have responded to this plagiarism). Within Whitehall there were essentially two interpretations; the Bank of England interposed a third.

From 10 Downing Street Professor Walters had argued almost since he took up his post in the winter of 1980 that the Treasury was aiming at the wrong target. In the spring and summer of 1981 he had campaigned for monetary base control. This was fiercely opposed by the Bank of England, since it was liable to involve – as arguably it had under Paul Volcker at the US Federal Reserve – excessive volatility in interest rates. The Bank's concern was that the marketing of government debt would be dangerously disrupted, and the market operators – in particular the discount houses – discomfited or worse. But apart from that, steep rises in bank base rates, which would from time to time have arisen from monetary base control, would feed back on to mortgage rates charged by the building societies; and the politicians – and first and foremost the Prime Minister – would not have stood for that. So Professor Walters lost that battle.

He then turned his attention to the narrow monetary aggregate, M1, arguing that this gave a better guide to what was really happening to money and to inflation prospects. It was in some respects a paradoxical position for him to adopt, since he had argued vociferously in the early 1970s that the explosive growth of £M3 was signalling inflation to come, when the Heath Government had been seeking to concentrate attention on M1, which happened to be performing a good less exuberantly. Now the experience of the early 1970s was being repeated (albeit on a much more moderate scale): while £M3 had been growing at an annual rate of up to 18 per cent, M1 had stayed in modest single figures. Professor Walters had switched sides.

The official Treasury was more cautious. But it, too, felt that £M3 was giving a misleading signal, being boosted by a propensity of the private sector to accumulate money assets which were perhaps relatively stable, and thus unlikely to give an early boost to domestic inflation. So while there was caution about following the Walters line that M1 was all there was to worry over, there was a disinclination to contemplate the sort of rise in interest rates which would have been needed to bring £M3 back on course.

This was certainly convenient. Another rise in interest rates would have exasperated the CBI and the Tory backbench critics. It might also have led to some reversal of the fall in the exchange rate for the pound which had occurred in 1981, and which appeared now, for the time being, to have stabilised. And the Bank of England – and in particular the Governor, Gordon Richardson – argued passionately for exchange rate stability.

But the Bank did not content itself with propagating an abstract case for exchange rate stability. When he visited the United States, Governor Richardson campaigned publicly for coordinated central bank intervention to bring the exchange markets to heel; at home he argued vigorously, against a wall of scepticism at the Treasury, in favour of more aggressive action by the Exchange Equalisation Account; and, in view of the refusal of the US administration to have any truck with a wider management of parities, the Bank became the champion of full British participation in the European exchange rate grid.

This was a controversy with a lengthy pedigree. When the first attempt to establish a regulated relationship between the national currencies of the European Community (the so-called 'snake') was mounted in the early 1970s, Britain had briefly joined. But at the time the Heath Government had just embarked on an ambitious programme of expansion, and the pound had come under heavy market pressure. After a few brief weeks of heavy intervention to sustain the currency, it was withdrawn again; and in due course the 'snake' collapsed.

Then, towards the end of 1978, the German and French Governments had promoted a new and considerably more complex system of coordinated intervention to stabilise the parities between Community partners. Britain agreed to become a founder member of the new European Monetary System, and to participate in a partial pooling of national currency reserves. But Chancellor Healey drew back from participation in the exchange rate mechanism, or grid, essentially because the Labour Government did not want to forgo the freedom to try to sustain competitiveness by debasing the currency. Paradoxically, had sterling joined the grid when it was formed early in 1979 it would have created intolerable strains not by weakness, but by strength.

The incoming Tory Government espoused an attitude of wait and see: its intention, as Sir Geoffrey Howe reiterated, was to sign up with the grid when the time was ripe. This position embraced, as was easily surmised, a diversity of attitudes. The Bank of England, inspired by the pursuit of stable parities, constantly campaigned for participation. So did the Foreign Office, though for rather different reasons: it fondly imagined that full British membership of the EMS would soften our partners' response to the Prime Minister's demands for 'our money back', which otherwise promised trouble. The Treasury was divided. Its departmental instincts were anti-European, and indeed isolationist: 'abroad' was one of the many locations where British Governments squandered money. Such instincts were reinforced by the attitudes of Foreign Office and Bank: the Treasury naturally distrusted the preferences of both the other institutions, and when they happened to agree there was a strengthened predisposition on the part of the Treasury to assume they must be wrong.

More fundamentally the Treasury argued that, as a petro-currency, the pound was liable to be subjected to precisely inverse pressures to those impinging on the continental currencies when major shifts in world oil prices occurred (the Bank argued, with more faith than logic, that large oil price movements were behind us). It also argued that for a government committed to the proposition that monetary control was the precondition for achievement of its first priority, the abatement of inflation, it would be paradoxical to tie sterling to a grid which might oblige the Bank of England to boost domestic liquidity when the domestic signals suggested there was too much of it about, or to squeeze it when it was already looking tight.

Yet officials were shifting slowly, and ministers more so. As Financial Secretary up to September 1981, Nigel Lawson had flirted with the attractions of tying sterling to the deutschmark in the expectation that the German currency would be rising, and thus helping to choke off a revival of inflation expectations at home. Other ministers argued, on the contrary, that Cabinet resistance to Treasury calls for higher interest rates would be stiffened if the justification for such calls consisted of obligations to the European Community rather than domestic credit conditions. But by the beginning of 1982 the volume of external criticism of the Treasury for alleged indifference to the repercussions of exchange rate movements on the health of the 'real economy', reinforced by complaints about the autumn rise of interest rates in 1981, had got under the departmental skin. The mandarins might not yet be persuaded of the merits of a fixed pound–deutschmark relationship; but the joys of free (or even dirty) floating currencies had faded.

To the certainties of Bank and Foreign Office, and the growing uncertainties of the Treasury, however, there was one firm answer. The Prime Minister's instincts were not sympathetic to entanglement in a continental currency relationship: and her instincts were fiercely reinforced by the opinions of Professor Alan Walters. Number 10 would have no truck with EMS full membership.

That did not mean that the exchange rate was destined to resume its role as a residual. If the Bank of England was not allowed to join the European exchange rate mechanism, it continued to set its heart on stability for sterling, always eager for intervention, and urging action on interest rates if pressure grew in the exchange markets either way. The Treasury was more concerned to prevent any recrudescence of sterling appreciation: it was relaxed, almost to the point of cheerfulness, about sterling weakness. Professor Walters took a closely corresponding view; but while the Prime Minister continued to object to high interest rates and their repercussions on the mortgage rate, she did not share the cheerfulness when sterling plunged.

Such was the background to Sir Geoffrey Howe's fourth Budget. It was widely seen – and welcomed, often caustically, by the backbench voices of dissent – as marking a decisive break with the monetary 'rigidity' of previous years. That interpretation, like the rigidity supposedly preceding it, was overdone.

That there was a significant relaxation in monetary policy would be difficult to dispute. In the year just ended it was calculated that £M3 had grown by 14½ per cent: a full 4½ per cent above the top end of the target range selected in the 1981 Budget. But far from there being any attempt to 'claw back' (in the phrase of former Financial Secretary Nigel Lawson) the overshoot, it was decided to lift the target for the coming year to 8–12 per cent. Moreover this range was to apply not just to £M3, but also to a broader aggregate, PSL2, which included deposits with the building societies, and to the narrow aggregate M1. And it was specifically acknowledged that if, as was hoped, inflation and interest rates contracted, then M1 might well shoot out of the top end of the range (since as interest rates fell the public were liable to be less concerned about leaving cash in their current accounts) without any cause for concern. 'On the other hand', the Red Book added, 'further changes in the terms offered on transactions and savings deposits could affect the relative size and significance of different measures of money.' In short, the Treasury proposed to suck it and see – taking account 'of all the available evidence, including the behaviour of the exchange rate'.

The justification advanced for this more relaxed posture was that the behaviour of £M3 in 1981/2 had been distorted, first by the civil service strike, and then by the move of the banks into housing finance. To the extent that the banks were simply substituting for the building societies, £M3 was boosted, although the 'real world' was unchanged (in fact – which the Treasury understandably did not acknowledge – the banks were to a considerable extent coming up with *additional* lending). 'The balance of the evidence', the Treasury concluded, 'suggests that, as intended, financial conditions have been moderately restrictive during the past year.' The price of fixed assets such as housing had been flat; interest rates had been high; the exchange rate had stayed 'at or above its May 1979 level'; and money GDP (a new and suddenly fashionable concept embracing both volume growth and change in money values which suffered as a yardstick of economic performance only from the impracticability of ascertaining what it was doing at any given moment) had undergone a 'sharp deceleration'.

Fiscal policy was also eased. The major changes in the Budget were a 1 per cent cut in the national insurance surcharge, the payroll tax introduced by Denis Healey, which had become a prime target of the CBI, and an increase in tax allowances of 2 per cent more than inflation since the 1981 Budget; in addition Geoffrey Howe went some way to redeem one outstanding Tory manifesto pledge by excluding future growth in the value of assets which reflected only the debasement of the coinage by inflation from capital gains tax. The result was estimated to be a loss of £1.5bn of revenue in 1982/3, and of £2.5bn in future years, over and above the balance which would have been struck by the indexation of both tax allowances and indirect taxation. This would mean a Budget deficit of £9½bn, or £1bn less than the expected outturn for 1981/2, and equivalent to about 3½ per cent of national resources, 'much as suggested' in 1981 (actually ½ per cent more). Public expenditure as a proportion of the GDP would be marginally less than in the previous year; there would be a £4bn surplus on the balance of payments; inflation would fall to 9 per cent by the year's end and to 7½ per cent by mid-1983; and output would grow by 1¾ per cent for a year, and then by 2½ per cent a year for the next two years. It was, said Sir Geoffrey, 'a Budget to help commerce and industry help itself'.

The reception was just about as good as the reception given to his previous offering had been bad. The inflation, output and balance of payments forecasts were greeted with extensive scepticism, and the Opposition and the Keynesian critics on the government backbenches dismissed it all as tinkering while the industrial heartlands died. But Sir Geoffrey had contrived to give satisfaction to a wide range of interest groups – industry with the payroll tax cut, the City with forward indexation of capital gains (although there were to be bitter complaints about its complexity), the Scots with increases in whisky and petrol duties which stopped short of full indexation, the small business lobby with a special 'enterprise package' – and an extensive programme of pre-Budget consultations with the Tory backbenches had paid off.

There were, however, two potholes on the road ahead. One was that one month after the Budget, in April, the Treasury discovered that the previous year's deficit had not been £10½bn after all, but only £9½bn. This was largely because the last forecast of borrowing by the local authorities before the Budget, completed with nine months of the financial year gone, turned out to have been a wild overestimate. It meant, of course, that if the predictions for spending and for revenue in the year ahead proved correct the PSBR would not be on a declining path as promised. Those who complained about the Treasury's 'obsession' with the PSBR were quick to claim this as proof positive of its unpredictability (which in fact the Treasury had always emphasised). But outside the Treasury, where inevitably this belated discovery caused some heart-searching, the revelation was largely ignored and very soon forgotten.

The other pothole was more serious. Back in 1980 the Chancellor had announced his intention to take short-term sickness and unemployment benefits into tax. There was nothing very revolutionary about that. Right from the inception of the comprehensive Welfare State in 1948 it had always been intended that such benefits should bear tax like other forms of income; hitherto it had not been found administratively possible to fulfil the intention. Ways had now been found around the administrative difficulties. Still, tax could not be applied immediately, and so Sir Geoffrey had decided that meantime the annual uprating of these benefits to allow for inflation would be 'abated' by 5 per cent. In the autumn of 1981 the tax net had finally been extended. But the 5 per cent abatement was maintained.

Backbench dissenters had become increasingly indignant about what they regarded as a breach of undertakings given when the 'abatement' had been introduced. Sir Geoffrey stood his ground. Had the reception to his Budget generally been a repeat of the response to the 1981 Budget, the government could easily have been beaten. As it was, the determined rebels on the backbenches soon discovered that while the Opposition benches would be only too delighted to follow them, their own would not (the fact that the key amendments to the Financial Bill were reached in the immediate aftermath of the recovery of Port Stanley did not help their cause). They withdrew to fight another day – which they were plainly determined to do. The issue of the 5 per cent 'abatement' became to some extent the rallying-cry of the 'wets' in the closing year of the 1979 Parliament. Plainly the Prime Minister's position was now unassailable, and their warnings of awful electoral retribution, so convincing just a year before, would now have sounded absurd. A narrower argument over Treasury 'callousness' enabled them to advertise their unchanged status while awaiting better times.

10 Coasting Home

1982 was not a vintage summer. But for Mrs Thatcher and her government, the sun was shining. The departure of Lord Carrington (together with two of his subordinate ministers, Humphrey Atkins and Richard Luce) had necessitated another Cabinet reshuffle. Francis Pym, denied the confirmation of his shadow role as Foreign Affairs spokesman when the government was first formed by the claims of Lord Carrington, now achieved his ambition. It gave him little satisfaction. The Prime Minister distrusted the Foreign Office, which she regarded as quite inadequately robust in defence of British interests. Lord Carrington had kept her distrust at bay with a mixture of humour and insouciance. Francis Pym was not so well equipped, withdrawing in gloom and pain from many a rough encounter. But his own successor as Leader of the Commons, John Biffen, was well chosen. A quintessential 'House of Commons man', with as many friends and indeed admirers on the Opposition benches as behind him, he had now, perhaps for the first time, found his niche. Biffen's replacement at the Department of Trade, Lord Cockfield from the Treasury, supposedly owed his preferment to the need to replenish the ministerial bench in the House of Lords. But he was also consciously seen as an extra Cabinet ally for the Prime Minister. His relative innocence of the rough world of party politics was to prove a complication. Still the general balance of the Cabinet was little changed.

What mattered, however, was that at long last the fruits of John Biffen's 'three years of unparalleled austerity' were beginning, very tentatively, to mature. Unemployment continued to edge upwards, more slowly but inexorably, reaching a peak of almost 3.3 million in August; and though Norman Tebbit described this as 'somewhere near the plateau, somewhere near the top', few believed him. But inflation was now

125

falling rapidly: in the three months from July to September prices, helped by an abundant harvest, did not rise at all, and the Treasury's Budget-time forecast of the year-end RPI, dismissed at the time as wishful thinking, was beginning to look excessively pessimistic.

Meanwhile across the Atlantic the stern counter-inflationary monetary and interest rate policies which had been pursued by the Chairman of the US Federal Reserve Bank, Paul Volcker, since his appointment by President Carter, were suddenly, if tacitly, abandoned. It was explained (rather as the British Treasury had explained its more relaxed approach to monetary targets in the spring of 1982) that the signals given by the US monetary aggregates had become distorted by changes in financial markets. The real reasons for the change of tack were different. The US Government was suddenly confronted with the threat that a number of Latin American Governments, led by that of Mexico, which had borrowed massively from commercial banks in the 1970s, could not meet their obligations. Yet if their loans to the sovereign borrowers south of the Rio Grande became 'non-performing' the reserves of a number of the leading US banks would be wiped out. Moreover several major US corporate borrowers were hovering on the brink of bankruptcy. Rescue packages for both sovereign and corporate borrowers were drummed up; but the Federal Reserve could see that if US interest rates were allowed to jump as they had done in response to bad American money supply figures, the rescue packages could prove unavailing. So that could not be allowed to happen. American domestic inflation was shrinking rapidly towards zero. Paul Volcker adopted the slogan pressed on President Johnson by Senator Aiken of Vermont in the Vietnam War: 'say we've won, and get out'.

This had its implications for British interest rates. In theory, in a world of floating exchange rates, domestic interest rates should be guided by, and reflect, domestic monetary conditions. In practice a sharp divergence between US and British rates was liable to feed back onto sterling, and thus, in an open economy such as ours, onto inflation expectations. Now, with the government's funding programme proceeding smoothly, and the domestic money figures promising to behave more consistently with the Chancellor's target range than at any time since the administration took office, the news from the US Federal Reserve removed the last barrier to lower interest rates. In July and August the banks' base rates were cut by 2 per cent in four stages, and led by government gilts the stock market took off.

The government's most notable successes in the late summer and early autumn of 1982, however, were achieved in the arena of industrial relations. The pressures of recession, first in the UK in 1980–1, and then worldwide from 1981 onwards, had dramatically reduced the expectations and the bargaining power of trades union organisers in the private sector. Industrial disputes had shrunk to levels not experienced since the Second World War. But the public sector, tightly unionised and basking in the privilege of monopoly, had proved a great deal more intractable. The lengthy steel strike in the early spring of 1980 had ended with the relaxation of the financial targets fixed for the Steel Corporation to meet the union's claim. Whether those who continued to be employed by the Corporation made good, in real post-tax terms, the earnings that they lost by striking is hypothetical; what is not hypothetical is that thousands of them lost their jobs as customers found and stayed with rival suppliers. But the union saved its face, if not its power to fight another day.

The far more lengthy civil service strike in early 1981 produced a rather different balance sheet. The cost in terms of government expenditure – in this case revenue foregone for good – was greater. The cost to employees in terms of lost employment was negligible or non-existent: civil service employment was shrinking under government pressure; that went on regardless. But in this instance all that was shown from six months' selective disruption was an extra half per cent on the original offer, and the promise of a new and more broad-based enquiry to replace the system of 'comparability' with wages in the private sector whose withdrawal had provoked the strike.

The summer of 1982 produced two important strikes in the public sector, and a settlement that was arguably more significant than either. The strikes affected rail and health. The railways dispute was *sui generis*. British Rail was afflicted by a court of appeal for wage disputes presided over by one Lord McCarthy. Since Lord McCarthy was one of the TUC's in-house academics, from BR's point of view this was a little akin to contracting out the catering to the Borgias. But even Lord McCarthy had been obliged to concede that there were aspects of the manning rules applied by ASLEF to sustain its membership roll which were verging on the bizarre. So it had been agreed that the wage award – which BR had said it could not afford – imposed in the spring of 1982 should in part be hypothecated on single-manning of the driving cab, to which ASLEF was rigidly opposed.

When BR attempted to enforce this condition, a strike rapidly developed. For the first time since 1955 the nation's railways ceased to run. As with the steel unions in the spring of 1980, the railway unions were confronted with the unpalatable news that the nation seemed to be getting by without them. But in this case the dominant rail union, the NUR, hated ASLEF, and was seen by the moguls of the TUC as far more *kulturny*. So ASLEF was effectively isolated, and rapidly forced to beat retreat. At TUC headquarters the air was thick with charges of betrayal.

The other major strike of 1982 was a more traditional affair, involving the Health Service unions, CoHSE and NUPE. Conscious of the evil odour into which the unions had fallen with the general public during the 'dirty jobs' strike in early 1979, care was taken on this occasion to limit the duration and extent of disruption by calling what the French call *greves tournantes*: intermittent days, and then weeks, of stoppages designed gradually to tighten the screw. Both the unions and the Labour Party believed that public sympathy – always quick to line up behind the nurses in particular – was against the government. But the effectiveness of these tactics was diminished by the refusal of the non-TUC-affiliated Royal College of Nursing to take strike action; and sporadic 'days of solidarity' by other public sector unions, culminating in a 'national day of action' in late September met with an unimpressive response. After many long weary months of trench warfare the government did marginally improve the terms of its original wage offers, particularly for the nurses who had declined to strike, and promised another long-term comparability body similar to that offered to the civil service the year before. On the strength of these offers the unions finally and reluctantly called it a day, without much attempt to disguise their disappointment at the outcome.

The most significant contest of all, however, was the one that did not take place. In 1981 the miners had elected Arthur Scargill, the Yorkshire miners' leader, to succeed Joe Gormley as their President. Scargill was already a legendary figure with the 'broad left'. His finest hour had been when he had despatched his Yorkshire shock troops to besiege the Saltley power station in Birmingham during the 1972 miners' strike. His election to the presidency of the NUM, by an impressive majority, sent shivers down the spine of Whitehall. Yet one of the ministers closely involved commented at the time of his victory 'we shall see: but the NUM is a federation, where real power lies with the areas. Arthur Scargill may find he's lost his power-base.' That proved a prescient comment.

Scargill had campaigned hard for a strike to raise the Coal Board's pay offer in the autumn of 1981, only to lose the ensuing pithead ballot. But on that occasion he had had an alibi: Joe Gormley had not yet relinquished the reins, and had not attempted to hide his distaste for his successor's campaign. Scargill claimed he had been stabbed in the back. In 1982 there were no alibis.

Yet there were doubts whether the pitheads were in a more receptive mood for strike action against the 1982 Coal Board offer. The Scots, led by Scargill's Communist mentor Mick McGahey, would certainly vote for a strike – they always did. Scargill's own Yorkshiremen would presumably do likewise. But the 55 per cent positive response required by the NUM constitution was deemed a formidable hurdle. Stocks of coal at the power stations were large, and a strike would take months before it was likely to have a serious effect. Thanks to localised productivity bonuses the miners were high wage-earners, many of them now with mortgages and other long-term commitments.

So Scargill decided to try to broaden his front. He persuaded the National Executive of the NUM to couple the issue of pay with the emotive one of pit closures (although the Coal Board had abandoned its programme of comprehensive closures of uneconomic pits following the government's tactical retreat in February 1981, it had continued to negotiate individual closures of the biggest loss-makers). He then took his campaign to the individual coalfields. As the reports came in of packed halls and revivalist enthusiasm, gloom spread round Whitehall. It might take months for coal strike to bite, particularly since the government had encouraged the Coal Board to move stocks to the power stations. But memories of Mr Heath's fate at the miners' hands were fresh in everyone's mind.

The ballot was taken at the pitheads in the closing days of October; and almost at once reports began to come in (the secrecy of the NUM pithead ballot resembles that of an eighteenth-century parliamentary election) that Scargill was riding for yet another sickening fall. And so it proved. The miners voted by three to two against the strike call. The contrast between the successive routs inflicted by the miners' leaders on the Tory Government in the early 1970s, and the humiliating failure of Scargill's undisguised attempt to inflict a similar rout upon the Thatcher administration could hardly have been more glaring.

The art of successful government in a parliamentary system with a maximum life-span of five years is to make the painful adjustments early, so that there is something to show for them in good time to impress the voters. Modern British Governments had not proved very skilful at this art. In 1969 Chancellor Roy Jenkins had still been struggling to restore international confidence in the management of the British economy after the 1967 devaluation of the pound. In 1973 Mr Heath's boom had turned to dust and ashes in the collision with the unions. In 1978 Chancellor Healey's pre-election spending spree was ruined in the 'winter of discontent'. Whether by luck or good management in the autumn of 1983 it was beginning to look as if Mrs Thatcher had got her timing right. The unemployment situation remained as bleak as ever. But – to the immense frustration of the Opposition and the critics on her own backbenches – all the evidence of the opinion polls indicated that even the unemployed themselves were inclined to accept the government's message that while there were many reasons for their plight (the unions, failures of management, the world environment), government policy was a long way down the list.

There were still up to 18 months of the 1979 Parliament to

run, and Mrs Thatcher had firmly scotched all talk of a snap election to 'cash in on the Falklands factor'. So there was plenty of time for things to go wrong. Another oil crisis could wreck the prospects for recovery from the world and British domestic recessions (and while the danger of a third massive jump in oil prices was looking increasingly remote, given the weakness of world demand, the opposite danger of a price collapse and the break-up of the OPEC cartel was looming larger – a collapse which could have horrendous implications for the price of sterling and the government's oil revenues, as well as for the shaky economies of some of the other oil producers such as Mexico, Nigeria and Indonesia). Contagious default by a number of the 'sovereign borrowers' on their debts remained a gnawing anxiety: in October Dr Johannes Witteveen, a former managing director of the International Monetary Fund described the risk of an international banking collapse as 'undoubtedly higher than for many years past', and Sir Jeremy Morse of Lloyds Bank told the Australians that it was 'small, but not to be ignored', adding with mathematical precision calculated to chill the blood that it was '5%'. With President Reagan resisting all challenges to the sharp rise in US defence spending, and a Democrat-controlled House of Representatives resisting all assaults on welfare programmes, the US Federal deficit was spiralling upwards towards $200bn and beyond, and thus threatening to induce another jump in US interest rates, however reluctant the Federal Reserve might be to countenance it, leaving British interest rates and sterling dangerously exposed. At home, optimists on the Labour benches and among the economic commentators hostile to the government forecast that, come the winter, the trades union worm would turn at last: although after Mr Scargill's cropper that looked like wishful thinking.

There were also some awkward issues requiring government action. Relations between Europe and the United States were passing through a turbulent phase. The US farm lobby, hard hit by drought and recession, was demanding retaliation against dumping on third markets of the European Community's agricultural surpluses. The US steel industry was campaigning for protection against what it regarded as subsidised steel exports from Western Europe. The French, and other European Governments to a lesser extent, were outraged by the Reagan administration's insouciance towards the soaring exchange rate for the dollar, which was confronting France with unsustainable trade deficits owing to the pricing of essential imports, including oil, in dollars. But the immediate point of contention was a decision by the Reagan administration in the summer of 1982 to forbid not only US subsidiaries in Europe, but also European licensees of American patents, to supply equipment for the pipeline the Russians were planning to build to bring natural gas to central Europe. The American ban was provoked by the Russian occupation of Afghanistan and the threats of Russian intervention in Poland to put down the Polish free trades union movement 'Solidarity'; but it was also justified by the argument that the pipeline would make countries like Austria and West Germany excessively dependent on Russian energy supplies, and hence vulnerable to Russian blackmail. The US administration had in fact a respectable case in international law, since European firms manufacturing pipeline components under licence from US corporations had signed undertakings that the technology would not be incorporated in exports to destinations banned by US domestic legislation. Nevertheless the pipeline ban provoked a furious response in Western Europe, where it was regarded as a flagrant infringement of national sovereignty and – since the US administration had recently dropped the ban on American feed grain sales to Russia – sheer hypocrisy, and where its enforcement threatened a number of embattled engineering companies including John Brown on Clydebank. The Department of Trade embarked on legislation to require the UK manufacturers to defy the US ban, notwithstanding the prospect that if they did so they would be blacklisted in the United States and denied future access both to US patents and US markets. Fortunately there were many influential critics of the ban on the other side of the Atlantic, and eventually a formula was found to preserve the President's face and the European companies' contracts.

Nearer home the Treasury was already beginning to turn its thoughts towards the next Parliament. Now that a second term for Mrs Thatcher had suddenly become conceivable – even rather probable – it was high time to concentrate ministers' minds on where the trends of public spending were taking us. The Treasury's primary target was the defence budget. The government was committed to raising defence expenditure 'in real terms' by 3 per cent a year at least until 1985 in deference to objectives set for NATO. From the Treasury's point of view this was even worse news than it sounded. For it did not just mean that the Ministry of Defence was entitled to claim 3 per cent over and above the going rate of inflation. On top of that allowance had to be made for the fact that the cost of arms was rising faster than the general rate of inflation. 'Real terms' was interpreted to mean that the extra increment had to be taken on board as well. Furthermore in the aftermath of the Falklands triumph the Treasury had lost a foredoomed battle to have the cost of garrisoning and supplying the islands at the other end of the Atlantic subsumed in the existing growth allowance: and that meant an additional bill of some £5000m over the next four years.

On top of that there was the exponential growth of the 'demand-led' programmes of the Department of Social Security: pensions and unemployment and other welfare benefits, where the cost was determined by numbers expected to qualify multiplied by the commitment to maintain the purchasing power of the payments. There was also the cost of the Health Service, where an ageing population and rising life expectancy, coupled with the expense of medical sophistication, meant that the claim on national resources was liable to grow over and above the rate of inflation.

With a view to concentrating ministerial minds, the Treasury projected two possible paths for the gross domestic product over the rest of the decade and on into the 1990s. One extrapolated the actual growth rate since the first 'oil shock' in the early 1970s; the other, more optimistically, assumed that there would be a return to the rates of growth prevailing in the 1960s. Even on the more optimistic 'scenario' the extrapolation of existing spending programmes would leave no room for reductions in taxation unless resort were had to substantial borrowing, with the risk of rising interest rates and/or inflation. On the more pessimistic 'scenario' the prospect was one of large increases in the burdens of taxation. Ministers were invited to ask themselves whether such a prospect was acceptable; and if not, what they proposed to do about it.

The Central Policy Review Staff, or think tank, promptly obliged with some of its own suggestions. These were radical to a fault: primary reliance on private medical insurance in place of taxation and the National Insurance fund to meet the cost of health care; voucher schemes and student loans to trim the education budget; a shift from comprehensive (and earnings-related) national retirement coverage to self-financing occupation pension schemes for those in employment. They were also, unfortunately, sketchily presented. And they leaked. A full text of the think tank's thoughts appeared in the *Economist* newspaper.

The Cabinet took fright. There was, after all, an election looming up. The subject was erased from the Cabinet agenda without discussion, and publicly repudiated. Possibilities of improving the 'supply side' of the government accounts by broadening the tax base (eliminating tax allowances for institutional saving and house purchase, and narrowing the scope of VAT zero-rating) were similarly pigeon-holed within the Treasury. The most that could be done, it was concluded, until the election had been fought and won, was damage limitation: the avoidance of pledges of future behaviour in the field of public spending. Even this was only patchily successful.

The immediate outlook from Great George Street was a good deal more cheerful. Indeed the message from the soothsayers was that Sir Geoffrey's planned deficit of £9500m in the year to April 1983 was heading for an undershoot of at least £2000m, in part because of higher-than-expected oil revenues, and in part because of lower-than-expected spending, particularly by the local authorities on housing. This was viewed as something of a mixed blessing. Although it was the government's strategy to maintain the public sector borrowing requirement on a shrinking path, it was felt that an outturn of £7500m or less might be deemed excessively restrictive at a time when the economy was still deep in recession. So, however incongruously, while Chief Secretary Leon Brittan was hard at work negotiating with the spending departments to eliminate prospective overspending in 1983/4, Treasury officials were hard at work examining the scope for stepping up expenditure, or reducing revenues, in the current year.

What emerged was a judiciously-phased 'autumn package' involving an immediate cut of $\frac{1}{2}$ per cent in the payroll tax, with a further 1 per cent reduction to take effect in the following spring, and the concession to the drinks trade of a right to defer payment of duty for four weeks after release from bond. This was calculated to swell the deficit by about £1000m; in addition the Prime Minister and the Environment Secretary gave the local authorities a pep talk about the desirability of making full use of their spending powers for home improvement and construction.

Meanwhile it had also been decided to sweep away all remaining restrictions on hire purchase transactions. The car manufacturers had campaigned for the elimination of the discriminatorily severe restrictions which applied to the motor trade. But it had been felt for some time that to have restrictions on hire purchase at all was anomalous now that those with bank accounts and other credit facilities could borrow without legal constraint for consumer purchases – and considerably more cheaply than by hire purchase.

The assumption was that the abolition of hire purchase would give a temporary boost to late summer consumer demand, particularly for cars when the new registration suffix came in in August. That was its intention. But as the autumn wore on it became apparent that the boost was more than temporary; and when in November the building societies cut the mortgage rate by 2 per cent, something akin to an old-fashioned consumer boom developed.

The 1982 Tory Party Conference in Brighton was described as 'one of the quietest in years'. Pressures from the grassroots to turn it into a Falklands victory rally were firmly stamped on by the party hierarchy, always conscious of the danger of appearing to expropriate the achievement of the armed forces for overt party political advancement, and the Prime Minister, in her closing address, referred only briefly to events in the South Atlantic. But the expectation that this was liable to prove the last Party Conference of the 1979 Parliament (the favourite date for the election at this time was October 1983) would in any case have served to dampen dissent; and after Falklands, and with the Prime Minister and government riding high in popular esteem, the backbench critics had little choice but to keep their heads well down below the parapet. Home Secretary Willie Whitelaw came in for some rough treatment from the more vociferous grassroots for his alleged 'softness' on law and order: but this was by now an annual feature of his incumbency and the 1982 performance was a mild one by the standards of these things.

The CBI, which as usual followed the Tories to the seaside one month later, also delivered a familiar message. The recovery needed encouragement and consolidation. That involved, according to the leadership, three contributions from government: the abolition of the national insurance surcharge; statutory limitation of commercial rates; and a cheaper pound. As already recorded, Sir Geoffrey was about to go some way to meet the first request. The second – the 'capping' of the rates – was also viewed with sympathy by government. But Michael Heseltine's attempts to exercise tighter control on local authority revenue-raising had come up against fierce opposition from Tory backbenchers reflecting the lobbying of their local councillors. The call for devaluation of sterling went awry, being firmly rejected by a majority of the CBI's own conference.

It was promptly taken up in a very different quarter. Also in November Peter Shore, Labour's Shadow Chancellor, published his *Programme for Recovery*. This was, in some ways, a brave document and a considerable improvement on the schemes for huge increases in public spending coupled with large cuts in indirect taxation and interest rates and price control which had hitherto come from the Labour leadership and the TUC. Shore and his junior finance spokesmen had 'run their programme through the Treasury model' (in other words used a series of assumptions fed in through the House of Commons computer link-up to test the possible consequences of their proposals for employment, inflation, the balance of payments, etc.: the trouble, as the Treasury was quick to point out, was that the assumptions themselves were inherently questionable, begging as they did the likely reactions of the markets to a major change of economic direction). The main proposition involved a phased increase in public spending, rising from an additional £5000m in year one to an additional £18 000m in year five. The results of such a programme were shown to be fairly modest, with a marginal increase in the rate of domestic inflation set against a less than dramatic decline in unemployment. These results depended, however, on success in controlling wages: without that the prospect was for inflation soaring back towards 20 per cent a year and an unsustainable collapse in the balance of payments. Yet as some perceptive commentators noticed, control of wages would, under the Shore programme, be likely to lead to a surge in the profits of the private sector: arguably a most desirable consummation, but not one calculated to amuse his left-wing parliamentary and trades union colleagues.

Attention focused on none of these aspects of *Programme for Recovery*. It focused instead on the call (actually contained in an annexe to the main document rather than in the programme itself) for a 30 per cent devaluation of the pound, spread over two years. This was roundly attacked by government spokesmen and in the press as irresponsible, and openly questioned by former Labour leader Jim Callaghan. Shore withdrew, insisting that devaluation was no more than an illustrative option. But the damage was done: and not only to the Opposition.

For some time – indeed from soon after the abolition of exchange controls – the Treasury had worried about the impact of the next election campaign on sterling. The Labour Party was committed to a crash course of expansion (Shore's programme had been denounced on the left of the Labour Party as far too mealy-mouthed, and committing no one but its authors); and it promised to channel institutional savings into 'productive' investment in UK manufacturing industry. And the Labour Party was also – inevitably – committed to the immediate reintroduction of exchange controls. Institutions and individuals were thus served notice that if there were any serious risk of a Labour election victory they had better get their money out of Britain while they could: and overseas depositors in London, although they would not be caught by exchange controls, could easily divine the way the pound could be expected to move in such circumstances. Admittedly the opinion polls suggested that the prospect of a Labour victory at the polls was remote (and the capture by Labour of an ultra-marginal Tory seat in the centre of the deeply depressed West Midlands in November by a margin of less than 300 votes underlined the message). Nevertheless a switch of funds out of London as the 1979 Parliament drew towards its end was bound to look like a sensible – and relatively costless – insurance policy. Talk of a 30 per cent devaluation by an incoming Labour Government was quite enough to set the alarm bells ringing. Sterling got the jitters.

The appropriate response from government was not immediately obvious. The staff of the exchange control department of the Bank of England had been dispersed, and could not be swiftly reassembled. Admittedly the formal reintroduction of exchange controls (the enabling legislation was still in place in deference to European Community rules), coupled with the Bank of England's eyebrows might be sufficient to halt an outflow of domestically-owned funds for a time. But the impact of such a move on the confidence of foreign sterling holders would be profoundly unsettling: moreover it would be an embarrassing signal of political trepidation on the government's part. Yet the only readily available alternative, a sufficient jump in domestic interest rates to pull in short-term cash from overseas, would infuriate industry and dismay the Tory backbenches. Once again the option of tying sterling to the European exchange rate mechanism was canvassed; but the Treasury remained hesitant, and Number 10 flatly opposed.

For the first time the Prime Minister's determination to see her mandate through to October 1983 or beyond wavered. If the Opposition was going to play politics with the currency then the uncertainty would have to be eliminated by an early General Election. It was a skilful rejoinder. The thought of an early General Election terrified the Labour Party (although they naturally pretended otherwise). Devaluation became almost as much of a taboo subject on the Opposition benches as Harold Wilson had sought to make it back in the mid-1960s.

Market fears were not so easily disposed of. Unfortunately they coincided with signs that Paul Volcker and the US Federal Reserve were losing ground in their resolve to hold down US interest rates. Henry Kaufman, most prestigious of Wall Street gurus, warned that rates would harden: and harden they did. At the end of November British base rates rose a point to 10 per cent. The pound was steadied – but not for long.

Meanwhile the government had published the autumn forecast. It was cautiously optimistic. Inflation, after falling steeply since the summer, was predicted to fall further to below 5 per cent in 1983, and national output, after a tiny rise of a half per cent in 1982, was expected to grow by $1\frac{1}{2}$ per cent in 1983. Even so, unemployment was expected to go on rising: the Government Actuary's 'assumption', for purposes of calculating the calls on the National Insurance Fund, was that it would average 3.2 million in 1983. And the current account, after a surplus of £3500m in 1982, was expected to be in bare balance.

Attention, however, concentrated on another aspect of the autumn statement: the treatment of unemployment and supplementary benefits. As announced in the spring Budget, they were uprated by 11 per cent, reflecting the rate of inflation which had been predicted for the year to November. In the event, however, the actual rate of inflation had turned out at $8\frac{1}{2}$ per cent. Sir Geoffrey Howe announced that while the amount of the uprating of benefits due in November 1983 would be decided, as usual, at the time of the spring Budget, the 1982 overshoot would be recovered. He also firmly resisted pressures to take the opportunity to restore the 5 per cent deduction from unemployment benefit. The Opposition expressed outrage at such miserliness. In fact the Treasury was only following tradition: since it took several months to adjust benefit codes it was inevitable that the uprating, when it came, was higher or lower than the inflation outturn, and had to be corrected in the following year. Nevertheless the Tory whips were warned that if the Treasury proceeded with its intentions they would have a rebellion on their hands.

Shortly after Christmas the Prime Minister departed on an unheralded visit to the Falkland Islands. Even before her departure the pound had begun to slide again, notwithstanding comparatively large-scale intervention buying by the Bank of England. Inter-bank interest rates moved up in sympathy. The pressure for another rise in base rates assumed formidable proportions. Expectations of higher US interest rates, stimulated by weekly American money supply figures which largely exceeded the targets of the Federal Reserve, and by the prospect of a soaring US Federal deficit played a part. But the proximate cause of trouble was the fear that world oil prices might collapse, carrying sterling with them.

The Treasury found itself caught in crossfire. Resisting the market pressures might lead to a dizzying fall in the exchange rate, which even massive intervention by the Bank of England might be powerless to halt. Allowing base rates to rise again was likely to provoke a Prime Ministerial broadside as soon as her plane touched down from the Falklands. After some hours of agonising the Treasury was obliged to bow to *force majeure*. Base rates rose again. This time sterling steadied, and stayed steady.

The Prime Minister, however, was indeed displeased. Shortly after her return she was entertained by the chairmen of the clearing banks. It was, by all accounts – and a circumstantial account soon found its way into the pages of the *Financial Times* – a sulphurous occasion, during which the Prime Minister accused the banks of having engineered the rise in base rates to improve their margins. Their defence – that a government which professed to believe in market forces could not expect those forces always to work the way it wanted them to – notably failed to impress.

Nevertheless it was to the clearing banks that the Prime Minister turned to find a successor to Governor Gordon Richardson of the Bank of England. Governor Richardson's second term was up in the summer of 1983. All sorts of names had been canvassed for the succession, ranging from the Financial Secretary of Hong Kong, Sir Philip Haddon-Cave, to the Prime Minister's own adviser, Professor Walters. The Bank's own choice was said to have been Sir Jeremy Morse, a former Bank of England employee and now Chairman of Lloyds Bank. As it became apparent that Sir Jeremy was unlikely to find favour, it was reported that Mr Richardson himself would be prepared to serve for another three years. In the end the Prime Minister's choice fell on another clearing banker: Robin Leigh-Pemberton, Chairman of National Westminster.

It was something of a turn-up for the book. Leigh-Pemberton, a landowner who had trained as a barrister and come late to banking, had been a popular Chairman of

NatWest. But his previous exposure to the mysteries of central banking did not compare with that of Sir Jeremy Morse, and it was inevitably argued that his chief qualification was his past as a Tory Chairman of Kent County Council and his sympathy with the Prime Minister's philosophy. It took him a bit of time to adjust to the special attention the press was liable to pay to the comments of a prospective Governor of the Bank of England. But it was at least arguable that his gregarious and more relaxed approach to the role was what the Bank might need after the formidable and dominating presence of Gordon Richardson. Certainly the occasional tensions of the Thatcher–Richardson relationship were unlikely to recur.

That was for the future. For the moment the double jump in interest rates inevitably increased anxieties at the CBI, on the government backbenches, and indeed in the government itself, lest the shallow recovery might be aborted, and hence increased the pressures on the Treasury to produce an expansive Budget. Helped by the weakness of commodity prices inflation was continuing to fall and was now predicted to drop below 5 per cent for the first time since the 1960s in the early summer; the Chancellor's money targets were continuing to perform soberly; the exchange rate had stabilised at a level which responded to the appeals of the CBI chiefs (if not of their Indians); government borrowing, after the autumn package, was expected to come out on target. In short the Chancellor appeared to have more room to manoeuvre than in the run-up to any of his other Budgets.

There was, however, one cloud on the horizon. For many months world demand for oil had been weak. The winter of 1982/3 was a mild one in the northern hemisphere. OPEC tried hard to steady prices by slashing production. But speculation grew that prices could collapse: that the OPEC cartel would not be able to stand the strain, and that once it did there was no floor under the price until it reached the actual costs of extracting oil in the Persian Gulf.

The implications of a reverse 'oil shock' would be far-reaching. The payments balances of such major oil importers as Japan, Germany and France, and of some of the most indebted of the Third World countries – Brazil, for example, and Argentina – would benefit substantially. Generally world demand would be sharply stimulated as purchasing power hitherto earmarked for oil was released for other uses. Against this the oil producers among the Third World debtors – Mexico, Venezuela, Nigeria, Indonesia – were liable to be tipped over the edge into debt repudiation, with disastrous implications for the world banking system.

The implications for the British economy were similarly mixed. UK exports ought to benefit from the boost to world trade (although past experience suggested that our market share held up best when demand was weak). Since North Sea oil was priced in dollars in line with world market prices, UK consumers would stand to gain like others from cheaper prices. But in the UK case, government revenues would suffer severely unless the fall in oil prices were offset (as was likely) by a fall in the value of sterling against the dollar – which would presage higher import prices and inflation expectations. And if the oil price were really to fall to the marginal cost of Persian Gulf production, or anywhere near it, then most of the North Sea fields would cease to be worth exploiting.

So the conventional wisdom was that a modest fall in oil prices – to around $30 a barrel – would be welcome; but a big fall would be fraught with peril. It was against this background that OPEC decided to hold its spring 1983 meeting not in Vienna or Zurich, as had been its custom, but in London. Britain, of course, was not a member, and Energy Secretary Nigel Lawson went out of his way to emphasise publicly that North Sea prices and production levels were determined by the market and not subject to government control or manipulation. Unfortunately it rapidly became apparent not only that OPEC did not believe him; but also that if their cartel did break down and prices collapsed, they intended to lay the blame on London for declining to restrain production.

The London OPEC conference was a cloak-and-dagger affair. Fleet Street pursued the sheikhs; but for the most part the sheikhs stayed out of sight behind a comprehensive security barrier in their luxury hotels. Meanwhile the Department of Energy and its Secretary of State kept well away and apparently out of touch. There were perilous moments when rumour had it that Nigeria – notoriously strapped for cash – was about to break ranks in search of custom, and bring the whole cartel toppling round about. But in the end a fragile compromise, involving further curtailments in Saudi output, a modest cut in prices to the $29–$30 range, with observance of a similar range for North Sea output by a process of osmosis, emerged. Nobody thought it would hold. It did. Nigel Lawson was generally reckoned to have achieved a combination of public aloofness and private collusion with some skill.

11   Maggie May

The five-year parliamentary life-span decreed by the 1911 Parliament Act is something of a snare and a delusion. Convention has it that a government which travels beyond four and a half years has got itself 'boxed in', since thereafter it has no further options for deferment if it runs into squalls. Consequently most modern Prime Ministers who have not, like Callaghan in 1979, been drummed out by Parliament, or, like Heath in 1974, concluded that their options have been prematurely closed, have chosen to take their records to the country with six months to go. It is far from clear that when, as in 1964, government has used its full term, the voters have punished its prevarication. But politicians are often more swayed by legend than experience, and the dangers of running voluntarily over four and a half years command a wide acceptance.

A second entrenched convention is that autumn is the most propitious season for renewal of a mandate. Here again, the lessons of experience are far from conclusive: Harold Macmillan did indeed secure a third successive victory for his party in October 1959 and Harold Wilson successfully consolidated his majority in October 1974; but Lord Home failed – albeit narrowly – in October 1964; and Labour won a second term in March in 1966, as did the Tories under Anthony Eden in May 1955. Nevertheless the received wisdom is that autumn, with the electorate refreshed from its summer holidays and the Opposition deprived of its vital parliamentary platform for two long months prior to the campaign, is the time to go.

Unfortunately in recent years the press has not even been inclined to wait that long. By the late summer of 1978 the national press was rife with speculation that the Callaghan administration, which still had a year to run, would take its chances in the autumn. And by the spring of 1983 the head of

145

speculation had built up once again about a June campaign, just four years into Mrs Thatcher's mandate. All the opinion polls were reporting that the government was comfortably ahead of all its rivals; if it waited for the autumn – it was argued – the Falklands triumph would almost be forgotten, another looming conflict with the European Community over Britain's contributions to its budget might well be out in the open, cruise missiles would be arriving to the accompaniment of mass protest, and inflation would be taking off again.

Such speculation has proved remarkably difficult for Prime Ministers to manage. If they decline to be drawn, this only feeds the speculation, and very soon they find themselves accused of indecision. If on the other hand they issue a firm rebuttal they are liable to face the charge of taking fright – and, more important, they close their own options.

All the signs were that Mrs Thatcher's own preference was to defy the fashion and carry on until the spring of 1984. She was sensitive to allegations – loudly levelled by the Labour Opposition, desperate to put off what they shrewdly foresaw as an evil day for them – that an early election would amount to 'cutting and running' to capitalise on Falklands and on the (strictly temporary) dip in inflation below 5 per cent. Her instincts told her that perseverance to the end, or very near it, would be more in keeping with her reputation for resolution. Besides, when she spoke of her broad strategy requiring at least two Parliaments she meant two full five-year terms, not terms cut off before their allotted life-spans.

The majority of her closest colleagues and advisers did not fancy soldiering on to 1984. Some of them were already pressing the case for a late spring election; most adhered to the conventional choice of autumn: and gradually this predominant preference appeared to be making headway against the Prime Minister's own inclinations for deferment. Labour's hasty retreat from its 30 per cent devaluation option, coupled with the sharp fall in sterling that had actually occurred during the autumn, had taken most of the effectiveness from the argument that Opposition irresponsibility necessitated an early election to resolve uncertainties in the foreign exchange markets; but by the same token the depreciation in the exchange rate threatened a renewed surge in inflation from the late autumn onwards. At any rate when the Prime Minister addressed her backbenchers in March she left them with the firm impression that October was indeed the month ringed round in her diary.

So Sir Geoffrey Howe had to prepare his spring Budget on the assumption that it would be the last before the polls. It was, by common consent, far too late to hope to achieve a turnround in unemployment in time to impress the voters; but fortunately, if the opinion polls were to be believed, this might not matter very much. On the other hand with between £1000m and £2000m available to 'give away' in what could be construed as conformity with the guidelines of the medium-term financial strategy, there was a strong incentive this time to put the emphasis on bonuses for citizens rather than for business. Business, after all, had already been promised a double cut in the national insurance surcharge, and it was already enjoying the 'more competitive' rate for sterling for which the CBI leaders had clamoured.

Yet there was considerable sensitivity about a possible charge of seeking to 'bribe the electorate' which, it was believed on somewhat tenuous evidence, was liable to lead to retribution in the polling booth on a government deemed guilty; and hence much agonising about the achievement of 'balance' between rewards for industry and rewards for taxpayers. It was a somewhat artificial debate, for while taxpayers show a deplorable penchant for frittering away extra take-home pay on imported knick-knacks, some of the extra demand is certain to rub off on domestic suppliers; whereas while a proportion of reduced taxation on the corporate sector will be retained in higher profits and improved competitiveness, some is certain to seep out to higher individual earnings.

Electoral calculation was not the only complication to Sir Geoffrey's sums. There was also the gnawing uncertainty about what was going to happen to the oil price. In 1982 Sir Geoffrey had served notice in his Budget speech that if petroleum revenues failed to match up to expectations because of falling prices, he would 'stand ready' to take corrective action in the autumn – although whether this was to take the form of application of the 'regulator' to raise indirect taxes, or of a mid-year axe to public spending programmes, he shrewdly did not specify. In the event the oil price had stayed fairly firm, and it had been sterling that had weakened, leading to a rise in revenues from oil (for which the government had duly compensated with both reductions in taxation and increased spending). This time the margin of error appeared to be far greater; and the possibility that the Budget arithmetic would have to be sent back to the drawing board remained open almost to the last moment.

In the end OPEC patched up its seemingly shaky compromise just in time, and Sir Geoffrey went ahead with a Budget which duly gave priority to tax thresholds. These were increased by nearly £1200m over and above the conventional adjustment for inflation. Excise duties, by contrast, were raised more or less precisely in line with inflation since 1982. There was a significant easing of the petroleum revenue tax burden on new and marginal fields to encourage North Sea oil development, and another judicious package of special tax concessions for small businesses. Tax relief on mortgage interest payments, which had been limited to mortgages of £25 000 throughout the lifetime of the Thatcher Government, was now extended to mortgages of £30 000. The vexatious 5 per cent 'abatement' of unemployment benefit was finally conceded – to give way to an almost equally contentious announcement that in future the autumn uprating of welfare benefits and pensions would be related, not to an estimate made six months in advance of the rate of inflation in the year to the time of uprating, but to the actual rise in inflation in the year ending in May, six months before the uprating took place.

The result of all these changes was reckoned to be that borrowing would be increased by some £1.6bn over the coming year; but that the total sums the government would need to borrow would amount to about £8bn (marginally less than the figure pencilled in for 1983/4 in the 1982 Budget). Inflation was forecast to rise modestly to 6 per cent by the year end, and to stay thereabouts through to mid-1984. Output was expected to grow by about 2 per cent in 1983, rising to $2\frac{1}{2}$ per cent in the first half of 1984, with still a further implied rise in unemployment, albeit at a much slower rate. The current account was predicted to be in surplus to the tune of £$1\frac{1}{2}$bn.

In general the Budget was well received. The Opposition

predictably concentrated its fire on the change in arrangements for calculating the uprating of benefits; but the effectiveness of the attack was diminished by recollections of the way in which Labour had made the change from retrospective to prospective calculation of inflation rates in order to save money in 1975. Tory criticism was muted by the abandonment of the 5 per cent 'abatement', and also by satisfaction at the sharp increase in the taxation threshold. But both sides of the Commons were increasingly conscious of the looming prospect of an early election campaign, and the Opposition made the most of the admission it drew from Treasury Ministers that over the lifetime of the 1979 Parliament, and in contrast with the government's election manifesto, the burden of taxation-plus national insurance contributions on all save the highest incomes had increased markedly.

More worrying for the Treasury's internal housekeeping was the discovery, within weeks of the Budget, that the deficit in the financial year just ending had not been some £2bn below the 1982 prediction, as Sir Geoffrey had told the Commons, but less than £½bn undershot. At first blush this might have been deemed a satisfactorily consistent outcome. Unfortunately it suggested an unforeseen surge in spending towards the end of the year which was likely to run on into the new financial year, and to shed doubts on the Chancellor's latest forecasts (and in particular the wisdom of reducing the unallocated contingency reserve to less than £1100m, while assuming that departments would underspend their budgets by £1.2bn, or £200m more than the latest estimates of underspending in 1982/3).

Parliament, government and press had other matters on their minds. Speculation about the likelihood of an early General Election was reaching fever heat; and just as Jim Callaghan had fanned the flames in the autumn of 1978 by inflicting a rendition of the old ditty about the expectant bridegroom ('there was I, a-waiting at the Church . . .') on the TUC conference, so Mrs Thatcher incorporated the words of another music-hall ditty, 'some say Maggie may, others say Maggie may not' (without apparently realising that the heroine of this particular epic had been a Liverpool tart) in her address to the CBI annual dinner in mid-April.

In reality her freedom of manoeuvre was closing in. At the

end of February the Liberals had captured a rock-solid London dockland constituency from Labour, with the Tory candidate losing his deposit. But this was widely seen as a freak result, attributable to Labour's choice of candidate (eccentric, even by Labour Party standards). A month later another by-election in Darlington produced a result much more in tune with the current opinion polls. Labour had narrowly beaten the Tories in 1979: now they consolidated their margin. But the Tory candidate came a very respectable second, with the Liberal trailing far behind. The Liberal–Social Democrat Alliance was in fact in some disarray, with public squabbling about whether Roy Jenkins, the titular leader, or David Steel, who stood far higher in the polls, would be their nominee for Number 10, when the evidence suggested that the choice was most unlikely to arise.

Elsewhere the omens for the government looked increasingly propitious. Arthur Scargill, nothing if not a glutton for punishment, once more called upon his members to vote for strike action, hoping that on this occasion the Prime Minister's decision to appoint Mr Ian McGregor, denounced by union militants as a 'butcher' of the Steel Corporation, to run the National Coal Board would reinforce resistance to the Board's latest plans for pit closures. Yet again the membership spurned its leader's call, this time by the solid margin of 61 per cent to 39 per cent. On the other side of the fence the CBI, which had played the sceptic about the recovery from recession to the government's irritation for so long, now confirmed that recovery was indeed under way. As if to underline the point the High Street banks cut their interest rates by a full point in two steps; and even the European Community seemed to give a helping hand. At the beginning of March the right-of-centre Christian Democrats had swept to power in Federal Germany, sending a signal of good omen to the British Tories; and at the end of the month the Prime Minister emerged from a summit meeting in Brussels to claim that she had extracted a 'firm commitment' from her colleagues to agree to another Budget rebate for Britain in respect of 1983 at their next session due in June.

The event which probably influenced the Tory Party managers more than any of these, however, was a bit of bad news: the routing of Malcolm Fraser's right-of-centre Govern-

ment in Australia. This was not because Australia was seen as
in any way a reliable pointer to the likely course of events in
Britain. Rather it was because Malcolm Fraser had called a
snap election well before his time was up in the belief that the
Labour Opposition leadership was unelectable. He might have
been right: only Labour promptly changed its leader, and
swept the country. Here the similarities with Britain were
potentially disturbing. Michael Foot, cultivated, witty and
generous of spirit, recognised in his time as one of the best
parliamentary performers of the age, had proved a hopeless
leader of the Opposition. Himself a natural rebel, he could
seldom bring himself to impose order on his bickering followers; and when he did try he made a disastrous mess of it.
Brilliant at the extemporary speech which winds up parliamentary debate, he regularly failed to master the material
needed to open debate as he had to do as Opposition leader.
With all his personal sympathies engaged on the side of the
unilateralist far left of his party, he encouraged the ambitions of
the militants. To the country at large he appeared an ageing,
confused and potentially dangerous old windbag. Tory Central
Office saw him as a major electoral asset.

They were not alone. As the election loomed nearer there
were regular reports of plots among the union barons to ditch
the Labour leader in favour of a more saleable alternative.
These rumours were as regularly denied; and in any case the
cumbersome electoral procedure with which Labour had
hobbled itself meant that a long and probably acrimonious
contest would ensue before a new leader could emerge. But if
the election were deferred until the autumn the possibility of
Peter Shore taking over or, arguably more alarming still, Denis
Healey assuming the leadership as tenant of the Deputy
Leadership – loomed large.

The Prime Minister still hesitated. Her instinctive preference for running long remained strong. But 'Maggie may'
dogged her footsteps, and there was some impatience on the
backbenches over the appearance of indecision. There
remained one final test. On 5 May England and Wales (though
not London, or Scotland) were due to vote in local government
elections. It was generally concluded that if these confirmed the
current message of the opinion polls (which gave the govern-

ment a lead of 5 points over Labour in mid-April) the Prime
Minister would have to overcome her scruples and request an
immediate dissolution. Broadly speaking, and with significant
regional variations, they did. Mrs Thatcher gathered her most
senior councillors to Chequers that weekend, and on the
Monday she bowed to their urgings. The country was to poll on
9 June.

It was a lop-sided contest. The Opposition had some success
in forcing the government on the defensive with a series of
'revelations' about Tory plans to attack the welfare state after
the election, and tensions within the Cabinet sometimes
surfaced – particularly when the Foreign Secretary unguard-
edly warned of the hazards of a massive Tory majority, to be
firmly snubbed by the Prime Minister. David Steel and David
Owen (though not Roy Jenkins) proved dangerously effective
on television. But for the Labour Party the election started
badly, and got worse.

Labour's lengthy manifesto, promising unilateral nuclear
disarmament, withdrawal from the Common Market, extensive further nationalisation, an end to the sale of council houses
to their tenants, and a programme of massive public expenditure coupled with cuts in interest rates and indirect taxation,
was harshly described as 'the longest suicide note in history'.
Labour canvassers on the housing estates were repulsed with
the allegation that they were 'nothing but a bunch of Com-
mies'. Such was the strength of the reaction on the doorstep
that Denis Healey, who was well known to dissent from the
pledge of unilateral disarmament, attempted to rewrite it in
mid-campaign. Jim Callaghan publicly attacked it as inconsis-
tent with the programmes on which the Labour Party had
fought preceding elections. By mid-campaign the conflicts of
policy and opinion within the Labour Party had become the
dominant topic of press comment, and the hapless Michael
Foot had to endure the ultimate indignity of a statement from
the party's General Secretary to confirm that he was still in
charge.

Given the vagaries of the electoral system, the hazard for the
government was not the performance of the Labour Party, but
the performance of the Liberals and SDP. In Scotland, the far
Northeast and the Welsh valleys, Labour was certain to make

the running. Elsewhere the danger of 'tactical voting', with disillusioned Labour voters writing off their party and voting SDP, and fair-weather Tories voting Liberal, was a real one. When it had happened before – in 1964, and more noticeably in 1974 – Labour had been the beneficiary, garnering its solid majorities in its Scottish, Welsh and Northeastern heartlands, while elsewhere voting fragmented.

The Tory vote held solid. It was the Opposition which splintered every way, with the Liberals and SDP combined only narrowly failing to overtake Labour in the popular vote. Yet because the Alliance support was broadly spread across the country, whereas Labour's was gathered in its bedrock territory to best electoral effect, the Liberals emerged with just four more seats, while the SDP lost almost all its MPs who had fought under a Labour banner in 1979, and returned with only six in all. Mrs Thatcher secured her second mandate, with precisely that landslide parliamentary majority – the largest since 1945 – that Francis Pym had warned against.

It was by any standards a remarkable achievement. Mrs Thatcher is the first Prime Minister to have been reelected at the end of a reasonably full-length Parliament since Salisbury. The Tories had secured 13 years of uninterrupted rule in the 1950s and early 1960s: but then they had taken the precaution of changing their leader for each contest with the electorate. Thenceforward it had become a canon of the received wisdom that the fickleness of the electors (or the inability of the elected to satisfy their aspirations) ensured that five years, or thereabout, was the natural life-span of a government. Mrs Thatcher had 'broken the mould' – and she had done so in defiance of the verdicts of Belgravia. The mixture of distrust, dismay and even contempt with which she was regarded in the salons had hardly been diminished by four years' experience. Hers was a double victory of the backwoods over the *bien pensants*. Was it deserved – or desirable?

12   A First Appraisal

'Under Labour, there has been too much Government interference in the day-to-day workings of industry . . . There has been too much government: there will be less.'

'We will reduce and reform taxation, giving first priority to reducing income tax so that people will keep a fairer reward for their work.'

'Our aim is to identify and remove obstacles that prevent effective competition and restrict initiative.'

This government 'is determined to control the growth of public expenditure so that its fiscal policy is consistent with its monetary stance . . . [it is] perhaps the first in Britain for very many years which has given monetary policy the importance it deserves.'

'Because we are observing strict monetary and fiscal policies if wage increases continue at the sort of rate at which they have been running . . . the result will be seen in rising prices, fewer jobs, lower output and more bankruptcies.'

The first Thatcher Government has been assessed, by friend and foe alike, as a major departure from the modern tradition of British political management. Hitherto the slogans and the banners changed, but the path, after brief post-electoral diversions, remained the same.

> The accurséd power which stands on Privilege
> (and goes with Women, and Champagne, and Bridge)
> Broke – and Democracy resumed her reign:
> (which goes with Bridge – and Women and Champagne).

But in 1979 the Lady marched in, banished bridge and champagne alike, and set off in a wholly different direction.

That there was a measure of convergence over the course of British politics from 1945 to 1979 is irrefutable. In 1951 a Tory

155

Government was elected to 'set the people free' from Labour's postwar controls and rationing. But Labour, in its last 18 months of office, had already – if belatedly – begun to throw the ration-books on the bonfire; it was Labour which had embarked upon the sharpest rise in defence spending in the postwar period (which the Tories speedily corrected); and it was the incoming Tory administration which appointed one of the two most accommodating industrial relations ministers of the postwar era in Walter Monkton. In 1964 Harold Wilson came to power on the programme of a planned and expanding economy: but it had been the outgoing Tory Government that had embarked on planning and expansion, in 1961. In 1970 Ted Heath displaced him with commitments to cut expenditure and better balanced budgeting: but in the previous year the outgoing Labour Chancellor had actually produced a budget surplus. In 1974 Labour took over once more to 'get the nation back to work' on the basis of a concordat with the unions: but the outgoing Tory Government had devoted its last two years in office to the search for precisely that concordat (even if, in the end, it had eluded it). Popular convention had it that Britain suffered from dramatic lurches between wholesale nationalisation under Labour, and *laissez-faire* Toryism. In practice the major shifts of policy had arguably occurred in mid-administration: to planning and a 'dash for growth' in 1961; to restraint of public spending and monetary targets in 1968; back to planning and another dash for growth in 1972; and then once more back to the axe and monetary targets in 1976.

1979, we are told, was different. This time the electorate chose – by intention or inadvertence – a government which not only promised to change course fundamentally, but also proved as good (or as bad) as its word. The Butskellite consensus, which was deemed to have long survived its authors, and to have taken not only Harold Macmillan, Alec Douglas-Home and Ted Heath to its embrace, but also Harold Wilson and Jim Callaghan, had finally been buried by the Lady from Grantham.

The Prime Minister lent some credence to this interpretation. 'Consensus' was not a sentiment she had much time for – indeed it was a concept which she publicly eschewed. Though she paid tribute to the continuity of the Tory tradition from Churchill through Macmillan, she notably omitted the Heath administration from the catalogue, as has been noted – to her predecessor's fury. And she inclined to hark back to an earlier tradition, of 'Victorian values' centred round self-help and the family. One of her senior ministers, Sir John Nott, even asserted that the government of which he was a member was nineteenth-century Liberal in inspiration, and not truly Tory at all. Dissenters on the Tory backbenches (and within the Cabinet) agreed with him.

The five quotations at the head of this chapter have been placed without attribution for a purpose. The first three might easily have found their place in the Tory manifesto for the 1979 election: but in fact they figured in the Tory manifesto of 1970. Similarly the last two quotations might have featured in speeches by Sir Geoffrey Howe or the Prime Minister: in fact they come from Denis Healey when he was Chancellor of the Exchequer. They are chosen to demonstrate the measure of continuity between the approach to government of the Tory Party in 1970, and that chosen in 1979; and also between the priorities in economic management of Denis Healey and Sir Geoffrey Howe.

Let us take the second proposition first. An obsession with the performance of a bunch of monetary aggregates is held to be one of the major, and fatal, aberrations of the 1979 administrations. In reality, of course, the revival of concern with monetary growth and its connection with inflation and the performance of the exchange rate dated back at least to 1968, when the International Monetary Fund, alarmed by the sluggishness of the convalescence from the 1967 devaluation with accompanying IMF support, felt obliged to send over a group to conduct a teach-in for the benefit of Treasury officials, to alert them to the significance of monetary constraint, which had been downgraded almost to the point of dismissal by the postwar neo-Keynesians. Thereafter Chancellor Jenkins had observed a target for domestic credit expansion (a yardstick which is designed to relate the rigour of monetary restraint to the balance of payments under a regime of fixed exchange rates) with such severity that he produced a rare budget surplus in 1969–70. After the 1970 General Election the incoming Tory

Government gradually abandoned monetary targeting, and by 1972–3 was acquiescing in a huge surge in money growth. Then, following Labour's return to power in early 1974 ministers (and some others) attributed the ensuing inflationary explosion to what Denis Healey liked to describe as his predecessors' 'monetary incontinence'; and when he in turn was forced to call in the IMF in the autumn of 1976, he accepted a commitment to the observance of annual monetary objectives. Sir Geoffrey Howe inherited the tradition.

True, Mr Healey was always something of a monetary chameleon. When he went to the City he made noises about the primacy of monetary policy like the quotation (from his Mansion House speech in October 1978). When he was speaking in the House of Commons he preferred to emphasise the primacy of wage control, and to construct simplistic relationships between the level of wage settlements and the inflation rate which he himself no doubt knew well to be nonsense. When he was addressing the trades unions he would summon up the ghost of social contracts past, and pretend to massage them back to life. But then Mr Healey has always believed that the purpose of public utterance is to titillate the audience: that it is what you do that matters, whereas what you say is virtually irrelevant. So it is more significant to note his actions: and of these the most significant was the decision to abandon the attempt to hold down the exchange rate in the autumn of 1978. This was a decision fiercely opposed by some of his Cabinet colleagues, and attributable directly to the desire to avoid a rapid surge in money growth. It was from that moment, and not from the return of the Tory Government seven months later, that the steep climb in the exchange rate to the dizzy heights of $2.40 began. The extent and nature of the incoming government's commitment to monetary policy requires separate analysis; but the claim that it was inventing a brand new instrument of economic management was quite unfounded.

The line of continuity between the approach to government of the Tory Party in 1970, and that espoused in 1979 is, admittedly, more superficial. On both occasions the theme was one of 'rolling back the frontiers of the state': 'our strategy', Mr Heath had told his first Party Conference as Prime Minister, 'is to encourage' individual citizens 'more and more to take their own decisions, to stand on their own feet, to accept responsibility for themselves and their families'. That was to become an even more familiar aspiration between 1979 and 1983.

But the motivation was in one ultimately crucial respect quite different. In its preparation for government before the 1970 election the Tory leadership had consulted widely in the business sector about the reasons for Britain's lacklustre economic performance. The message that came back was that government interfered too much, and taxed too much: 'Get the Government off our backs, and we will deliver the goods.'

So during the first twelve months of the Heath administration, as again in 1979, taxes were cut and public spending sharply pruned. But the goods were not forthcoming. Investment by the private sector did not burgeon, it shrank. Mr Heath felt personally betrayed. His ambition had been to restore the vigour and performance of the British economy. If the private sector would not seize the chance it had been offered, then government must take the lead. And so, from the early autumn of 1971 onwards, the retrenchment of state spending was put sharply in reverse.

His successor started from an identical standpoint. As she told Brian Connell on the first anniversary of her election victory, 'we want to build a country where people don't come to government for every decision, every house, every job, every pay increase, every price increase. That's not what made Britain the country she is. She has made the country she is [sic] by people being able to take their own initiatives and their own decisions. We want that throughout the economy and it's working . . .' But whereas to Heath the call to self-reliance was a means to the end of faster growth and improved industrial performance, to be replaced by something else when it did not appear to work – or at any rate to work within a tolerable time-scale – to Mrs Thatcher it was the only way forward: 'there is no alternative'. Another attempt to 'prime the pump' with a surge of public spending would be doomed to failure.

Yet here too there was a line of continuity, if not to Ted Heath then to Jim Callaghan. It had been Callaghan, not Margaret Thatcher, who had first pronounced the demise of neo-Keynesian demand management in his celebrated warn-

ing to his Party Conference in 1976: 'We used to think that you
could just spend your way out of recession and increase
employment by cutting taxes and boosting government borrowing. I tell you in all candour that that option no longer
exists; and that in so far as it ever did exist, it worked by
injecting inflation into the economy. And each time that has
happened, the average level of unemployment has risen.
Higher inflation followed by higher unemployment. That is the
history of the last twenty years.'

Labour came to regard that passage as a fatal aberration,
attributed (whether fairly or not) to the pen of Peter Jay,
Callaghan's monetarist-inclined son-in-law. But by the later
1970s scepticism about the effectiveness of deficits for economic
stimulation was not confined to enthusiastic monetarists. It
was the distinctly Keynesian Brookings Institute which had
concluded that of every £100 injected into the economy by
government in the middle 1970s, £92 had been dissipated in
higher prices or spent on imports. The added dimension which
Mrs Thatcher brought to this scepticism was the conviction
that it coincided with her own experience. In the world of high
street enterprise in which she had grown up, as she regularly
reminded her audiences, you did not prosper by going into
debt: nor would you dream of looking to the government to
perform a rescue if you did. What to Callaghan was a sad
confession of impotence (and one fairly soon forgotten once the
IMF had gone away) was to Mrs Thatcher a statement of the
obvious – but one that had to be hammered home.

Continuity, however, is no sufficient proof of virtue (any
more than radicalism is necessarily to be equated with vice).
The charge against the first Thatcher Government is that,
while it may have inherited the practice of monetary targetry
and modesty about the role of government, it pursued both
with a blinkered obsessiveness which ignored the plight of
British industry and commerce, and unnecessarily exacerbated
the severity of recession and unemployment. Critics on the left
and in the trades unions went further, and attributed to the
Prime Minister in particular a conscious strategy for unemployment to curb the power of union leadership (or, as they
liked to put it more euphemistically, 'the working man'). But
the Commons Treasury Select Committee not unfairly

reflected middle-of-the-road opinion when, in a report judiciously leaked (though incomplete) in the middle of the 1983 election, it attributed about half the rise in unemployment since 1979 to the world recession, the other half being attributable, by implication, to government policies.

What were these policies? Excessive stringency of monetary control, leading to excessively high interest rates, and a massive 'overshoot' in the exchange rate; the overzealous pursuit of shrinking budget deficits, leading to damaging reductions in capital investment; the abandonment of all controls on wages, resulting in a disastrous shift from retained profits to employment costs; the retention of the national insurance surcharge as a 'tax on jobs'; and the use of nationalised industry charges as a form of hidden tax calculated further to diminish the competitiveness of their captive industrial and commercial customers. In addition, critics on the right complained of a failure to curb the current spending of public services and local government; while those on the left denounced the abandonment of exchange controls for generating a surge of outward investment to the detriment of British industry.

That the impact of recession was relatively both swifter and more severe than it was in other advanced industrial countries cannot be gainsaid. Whereas the UK unemployment rate, at 5.7 per cent, was on a par with the French and American rates in 1979, and well below that of Italy, by 1980 it was on a par with Italy, and then rose far ahead of all the other major Western economies, which only began to show steeply increasing unemployment from 1981 onwards. Manufacturing output, which was broadly flat in Germany and France in 1980, and still rising strongly in Italy and Japan, fell by 8.5 per cent in Britain, and again by 6.3 per cent in 1981, when it also began to fall in Germany; and it was not until 1982 that all the leading economies apart from Japan were in retreat, by which time British manufacturing output, though still falling by another 1 per cent, was performing better than most of the competition.

But it would be as illogical to attribute the whole of the differential impact of the recession on British industry to policies pursued from May 1979 as it would be to attribute the whole of the surge of inflation in 1974 and 1975 to the Labour Government's 'social contract' with the unions. Between 1973 and 1978 unit labour costs in manufacturing in Germany rose by less than 40 per cent; in Japan they rose by 56 per cent; in the United States by two-thirds; in France by just over 80 per cent; and in the OECD as a whole by 62 per cent. In Britain they rose by more than 140 per cent – and this over a period when sterling had become sharply more 'competitive', not less. Meanwhile (and consequentially) the real rate of return in British manufacturing industry, which already compared most unfavourably with the returns obtained by Britain's major international competitors at the beginning of the 1970s, had fallen steeply further: to less than one-third of that available in the USA, Canada and Germany by the end of the decade.

The shrinking competitiveness of British industry was, of course, no new phenomenon. It had persisted on and off for a century. But it had accelerated dangerously in the 1970s. In the postwar period this erosion of competitiveness had been mitigated to some small extent, by design, inadvertence or *force majeure*, by the devaluation of the currency: by 30 per cent in 1949; by 14 per cent in 1967; and then, following the floating of sterling in 1972, by a further 15 per cent between then and 1975. In 1976 the rate then plunged by 17 per cent in a year. The mitigation was but modest, for any immediate gain in competitiveness was swiftly eroded by the rise in import costs and the spur this gave to domestic inflation expectations. Nevertheless the presumption became understandably implanted in the minds of wage negotiators that cost increases would be offset by adjustment to the value of the currency. Suddenly, towards the end of the decade, that presumption became misplaced. In the year to September 1978 the sterling/dollar rate jumped by a quarter. It is true that this reflected the generalised weakness of the dollar at the time: the German deutschmark, the French franc and the Japanese yen also appreciated against the dollar, and by more than the pound. But following the second 'oil shock' in the autumn of 1978 (and the Labour Government's decision to abandon the attempt to hold the exchange rate down) the pound began to appreciate sharply against the other major currencies as well. In the seven months prior to the General Election the sterling rate strengthened by 2 per cent against the deutschmark, by 6 per cent against the French franc, and by no less than 20 per cent against the yen.

Following the election the surge in sterling's value gathered momentum, with the trade-weighted average exchange rate rising 18 per cent to recover its 1975 value. The 'blame' for this appreciation can be split three ways, between the status of sterling as a 'petrocurrency', the conviction of the markets that the incoming government was determined to tackle UK domestic inflation, and the rise in UK interest rates. Of these the first was entirely outside the control of HMG (even if the government had somehow contrived to follow Sir Michael Edwardes's advice, and halted North Sea oil production, sterling would have been likely to reflect the suddenly enhanced value of the known and proved reserves of offshore oil). It might theoretically have been possible to convince the markets that the new government's reputation was unmerited, by embarking on policies plainly calculated to promote inflation; but such a course would have been perverse, to put it mildly. Only interest rate policy, therefore, could really be laid wholly at the government's door.

The respective weight to be attached to each of these three contributory causes must be anyone's guess. But at a time when speculation about the possibility of a further rise in world oil prices was rife, and when Britain alone among advanced industrial countries was self-sufficient in energy resources and endowed with a swiftly growing surplus for export, the 'oil factor' must have been a very substantial one in sterling's strength.

With benefit of hindsight, however, it is now fashionable to argue that the strength of sterling should itself have warned the Treasury that monetary policy was too tight. It seems a curiously circular argument. The level of interest rates, dictated by the desire to bring monetary growth under control, attracted foreign deposits into sterling. As a result the exchange rate rose. Because the exchange rate rose the government should have known that monetary policy was excessively severe. Yet in the first four months of the new government the target aggregate, £M3, was rising at annual rate of more than 14 per cent: at a time when some of the rise in sterling *must* have been attributable to petrocurrency appreciation it would have shown a remarkable indifference to the lessons of experience to read across from the exchange rate a message of excessive monetary stringency.

What can be argued with more plausibility is that the June 1979 Budget, in striking the balance between fiscal and monetary pressures to restrain the inherited inflation surge, relied excessively on the latter. A switch from direct to indirect taxation is inevitably front-end loaded, with the revenue recoupment delayed; and the immediate programme of reductions in expenditure relied heavily on economies in public service manpower costs which proved optimistic, and on asset sales which were really no more than an alternative method of funding the deficit.

The serious errors perpetrated by the incoming government – and they were serious – lay elsewhere, however. Essentially they were two. The first was the series of prior commitments given before the election on the public sector wages front – to the police, the armed forces, the firemen, and above all to Professor Clegg. The second was the scale of the shift from direct to indirect taxation in the first Budget. Their effects were most damagingly interconnected.

Each of these decisions, taken seriatim, was understandable. The Tory Party had made much of an ill-defined commitment to 'law and order' in the election: restoring morale and numbers in the police force by paying it over the odds was the most immediately tangible way of fulfilling that commitment. The same went for the armed services. As for the other public services, including the firemen, a repudiation of the Clegg comparability exercise and the deal by which the Labour Government had promised to keep the firemen in the 'upper quartile' of industrial wage-rates would have been bound to look like a gratuitous forfeit of their votes.

But even in an economy with a relatively efficient labour market the spectacle of pay being wholly disconnected from supply and demand in the public services would have given a jolt to expectations in the private sector. In an economy where years of experimentation with various forms of incomes policy had established the concept of a 'going rate' for each year's wage round regardless of ability to pay, it was asking for trouble.

The switch from direct to indirect taxation made matters far worse. In theory, of course, employees enjoyed a boost to take-home pay, and discretion to economise on VAT-bearing purchases so that they could have a wage increase without taking it out of the profits of their employers. The government hoped to underline the message by producing its 'tax and price index' and by emphasising that its commitment to monetary control would put jobs at risk if employees insisted instead on wage settlements to compensate them for what happened to the RPI. But governments had talked about irresponsible wage bargaining putting jobs at risk for years; and while unemployment had indeed risen inexorably from one business cycle to the next, monetary policy had invariably been relaxed, and the exchange rate allowed to slide, before things got really rough. Why should anyone believe it would be different this time?

There was an overwhelming case for the elimination of the confiscatory marginal rates of taxation which Denis Healey had imposed on higher incomes to placate the Tribune Group; and an almost equally strong case for a major increase in allowances to lift tax thresholds which had slipped sharply further down the income scale under Labour; and the consolidation of the assorted VAT rates introduced by Healey at 10 per cent, or even 12 per cent, to offset the impact of the essential income tax concessions on revenues. The crucial error was to cut the standard rate of tax from 33 per cent to 30 per cent. Unlike the tax threshold and the top marginal rates the standard rate was by no means out of line by international comparisons; and it took a feat of imagination to believe that 3p off the standard rate would transform the British work ethic. Yet it cost a prospective £1400m in a full year. Left alone, a consolidation of VAT at the existing 12 per cent higher rate would have been sufficient. The difference to inflation expectations, and hence ultimately to unemployment, would have been well worth having.

But first Budgets are usually composed in haste and repented at leisure. Denis Healey's first offering, in the spring of 1974, involved a monumental error about the liquidity of the company sector which he was forced to correct in the nick of time that autumn before the component companies of the *Financial Times* index went into collective receivership. In an ideal world we would have a law which forbade an incoming government to compose its own Finance Bill until it had been in office for six months, and the hot breath of the hustings had had time to cool. But we do not live in an ideal world. (One further lesson which might be drawn, not from Sir Geoffrey Howe's first Budget, but from those which followed, is that it is high time we reverted to the former practice of April Budgets. The arguments for March Budgets are that they give more time for parliamentary scrutiny of the Finance Bill, and that the Chancellor gets in an extra month of higher revenues from indirect taxes. With the abatement of inflation that second argument loses much of its force. Against this the Treasury is obliged to do its final sums with a whole month to go before the commencement of the year to which they will apply. As a result, in 1982 and 1983 we had the disturbing admissions, a month after Budget day, that borrowing in the year then ending had not been what the Treasury had said it was, by a wide margin. How many more times does this have to happen, one wonders, before Great George Street will see the light?)

When generous weight is attached to the sins of commission perpetrated by the incoming government in the 1979 Budget, and in its approach to pay in the public services, however, it is surely mind-boggling to deduce that they weighed equally with the legacy of wholly disproportionate increases in unit labour costs and vanishing profitability, plus the coming to maturity of the North Sea oil province at the very moment of the second 'oil shock', in the scales of responsibility for the differential severity of the ensuing recession in Britain – or anything like it. Had Professor Clegg been sent packing to the University of Warwick; had a couple of percentage points been shaved off the rise in the RPI in the winter of 1979–80 by a smaller jump in VAT rates; had more reliance been placed on fiscal restraint so that the minimum lending rate did not have to rise by five points in the summer and autumn, sterling would still have been rising strongly, and the 1979–80 wage round would still have produced a level of settlements necessitating mass redundancies. The sad truth is that if governments persist for long enough in the pretence that they can deliver full employment, the participants in the labour market will come to behave as if they could, and blithely disregard the warnings that the trick cannot be turned.

Unfortunately in politics myths are often more enduring than realities. The legend that the Treasury's indifference to the course of the exchange rate contributed largely to the severity of the British recession is now deeply entrenched, and it is scarcely surprising that the official Treasury itself should be increasingly vigilant to avoid a repetition. Were we to experience another 'oil shock', coupled with a sharp uprating of the pound, it is now a safe bet that the official Treasury would seek to bat it on the head with urgent cuts in interest rates and intervention regardless of the performance of the other indicators of domestic credit conditions. Whether it would succeed in reversing the instincts of the markets is another matter. The impact on home-grown inflation, however, could be unwelcome, to put it mildly.

At least it would not have to cope with another rather fundamental novelty about our circumstances in 1979–80 which critics of the first Thatcher Government often seem to disregard. In 1978, although North Sea oil and gas production and exports were swiftly building up, our trade in oil and natural gas was still in deficit to the tune of almost £2.5bn. By 1980, the deficit had shrunk to £400m; from 1981 onwards we began to run an accelerating surplus. In a world of floating exchange rates something else was bound to give. Either we had to purchase extra imports; or we had to export capital; or the exchange rate had to rise until our exports of oil or other goods were choked off, or sufficient outflow of capital was generated. For the accounts have got to balance. In practice the government did its best to promote a capital outflow by abolishing exchange controls – and succeeded in so doing, to the outrage of the Labour Party. Had it not done so it is hard to see how we could have avoided an even sharper appreciation in the exchange rate.

Before we leave the exchange rate traumas of 1979–80 it might be worth pausing for a moment to question whether the huge 'over shoot' in the sterling parity was altogether the disaster it has been painted. That it contributed to the brutal collapse of order books which hit British manufacturing industry in the spring of 1980 is not in contention. That it contributed to the transformation of inflation expectations which, by the late 1970s, were becoming engrained in the national subconscious is also beyond dispute. What is often overlooked is that currency appreciation transfers resources silently from producers to consumers, just as currency depreciation does the reverse. Since, in common with the other advanced industrial countries, our environment had been producer-dominated for the whole of the postwar era, currency appreciation was bound to come as something of a culture shock. Yet by definition producers represent a minority interest: from the cradle to the grave we are all consumers, whereas only those engaged in remunerated employment are producers. For more than 30 years the muscle-power of the producer lobbies – the CBI, the TUC and the various trade federations – had contrived to divert the politicians' gaze from this self-evident fact (and it is characteristic that arguably the most effective of the lot of them – in weight-for-numbers terms – the NFU, was able to insulate its members against the impact of currency appreciation). The sharp appreciation of sterling in 1979–80, may have deprived some one and a half million of the population of their producer status. But the combination of that appreciation, generous redundancy terms, and the abatement of inflation which followed, placed a variety of imported goods and foreign holidays within the grasp even of those who had been made redundant, often for the first time. The producer lobbies regarded it as axiomatic that the citizen offered a choice between a job and the ability to afford an Italian washing-machine would choose a job. Perhaps the outcome of the 1983 election proved them wrong.

Golden handshakes do not last for ever; and if currency appreciation led to permanent loss of total market share, with the accounts balanced by North Sea oil until it was exhausted, at that point we should all, as consumers, have to suffer the deprivation of overdue adjustment to the purchasing power of our money. But it is striking that throughout the postwar period the countries with the strongest currencies – West Germany and Japan – have achieved the largest gain in market share; while those with the weakest currencies – including

Britain – have suffered the largest erosion. It is true that no postwar economy (apart from the American, since 1980) has had to adjust to as *sharp* a revaluation of its currency as the one that Britain experienced in 1979 and 1980, and that at a time when Britain was at the top end of the domestic inflation table (but then the longer the addiction, the sharper the inevitable shock of withdrawal). Nevertheless experience suggests that an enforced concentration on the top end of the market, and the necessity to win orders on quality rather than price, does wonders for the performance of an advanced industrial economy; whereas the temptation to trade down created by a sliding currency does the reverse.

Give the government as much of the benefit of the doubt as you may for the burden of its inheritance, the world recession and the transformation of the pound's status thanks to North Sea oil; acknowledge the role that monetary restraint should play in the abatement of inflation; even make allowance for the errors of the June 1979 Budget. But having done so, there are many on what is usually described as the 'left' of the Conservative Party, and among Social Democrats and their ilk, who argue that some, at least, of the awesome increase in unemployment which ensued could have been averted had the government swallowed its pride and sought to come to terms with the trades unions. After all, the 1979 Tory manifesto had asserted that there should be 'more open and informed discussion of the Government's economic objectives . . . so that there is wider understanding of the consequences of unrealistic bargaining and industrial action'. And in *The Right Approach*, which had preceded it, approving reference was made to the German system of 'concerted action' to secure agreement about the affordable limits to each year's wage round. Yet in the event no serious attempt was made to add substance to these aspirations.

Now obviously had wage increases come to a grinding halt in the autumn of 1979 many hundreds of thousands of employees would have kept their jobs in 1980 and 1981 (although many hundreds of thousands would still have lost them); and some members of the government – most notably Jim Prior – did believe, as Robert Carr believed from the same department in 1970–1, that Conservatives could do a deal with union leaders to abate the strength of wage claims once the dust of the election battle had had a month or two to settle. The evidence was overwhelmingly against them. For while the Carr/Prior tradition was matched on the union side by occasional leaders such as Frank Chappell of the Electricians and Terry Duffy of the Engineers, who might have been inclined to talk terms seriously with the government, they were heavily outnumbered by those who – for understandable reasons – attached far more significance to their role as power brokers in the Labour Party than to their responsibility as patrons of their mass membership. After the second debacle which befell their party in 1983 there was indeed a change of attitude, since the prospect of sharing out the spoils of office with Labour had become remote. But by then the concept of a managed labour market had in any case passed into limbo. In 1979 the possibility of a concordat between the unions and a Tory Government, which had eluded the Heath administration, was a mirage.

Besides, the whole history of the recurrent attempts to apportion a 'national dividend' during the 1960s and 1970s had exposed its impracticability (and its disastrous repercussions) in a British context. Occasionally a wage freeze – as in the winter of 1972/3 – or a low flat rate limit on wage increments – as in 1975/6 – might succeed in postponing the full impact of inflationary pressures for a few months, but only to release them with redoubled force thereafter. Over any length of time there was no evidence that so-called 'incomes policies' had made any contribution to the abatement of inflation. On the contrary, because union leaders regularly demanded – and obtained – commitments from government to the pursuit of expanded deficit financing as the price of their complaisance, inflation expectations were exacerbated; while because the most powerful of those leaders tended to be drawn from unions with a high proportion of low-paid, unskilled (and usually underutilised) membership, they insisted also on a shrinkage of differentials which did long-term damage to the functioning of the labour markets. Worst of all, perhaps, they also claimed and were granted the right to formulate legislation designed to consolidate their own powers and the muscle-power of their officials at the grassroots over the ordinary union membership. Yet they had long forfeited the ability to deliver their side of any bargain: and indeed because the deals they struck with Labour Governments were so conspicuously motivated by their own self-interest, such authority as they yet retained was further undermined. By the middle 1970s 'social contracts' with the barons of the TUC had little more substance than treaties concluded with the exiled kings of Eastern Europe.

Most of the other charges levied against the 1979 government's strategy stick to the rhetoric rather than the performance. The publication of a medium-term financial strategy involving a steadily shrinking path for the budget deficit and monetary growth, without the semblance of a target for output, undoubtedly marked a clear break with postwar neo-Keynesian orthodoxy: a break which was spelt out bleakly in Sir Geoffrey Howe's presentation to the Commons Treasury Committee already quoted. But performance was a very different matter. Following a £1bn overshoot in the budget deficit in 1979–80, a massive £5bn overshoot was not only accepted in 1980–1, but justified on impeccably Keynesian, counter-cyclical grounds; and when, in the autumn of 1982, it was foreseen that the deficit was going to be some £2bn less than predicted, rapid action was taken to boost expenditure, notwithstanding the fact that recovery was well on course. As to monetary policy, the targets were regularly overshot – in 1980–1 by a huge margin – and then reset without correction for what had gone before. Only in the last year of the administration (when the unexpectedly steep fall in inflation meant that the target range of 7 to 11 per cent involved an unforeseen rate of increase in the 'real' money supply) was the target hit. Indeed there was more substance to the charge that, from the moment when the 'corset' was removed, and the true growth of money exposed, in the summer of 1980, the Bank of England consistently 'assisted' the money markets to hold down short-term interest rates, hence enabling the High Street banks to keep both the personal and company sectors plentifully supplied with credit, thereby going a long way to neutralise the essential purpose of monetary discipline.

It is true that, after the huge surge in government borrowing in 1980–1, the budget deficit, as a proportion of the national product, was steadily shrunk to one of the lowest levels in the world. But as Tim Congdon of Messels pointed out in *The Times* in May 1983, this really reflected no more than the consequence of the buoyancy of revenues from North Sea oil: disregard oil revenues and the 1982–3 deficit was the equivalent of 6.2 per cent of GDP in 1982, compared with 3.5 per cent in 1978. No doubt it would theoretically have been possible to use these 'windfall' tax revenues to boost welfare spending, as the Dutch had done with their revenues from natural gas in the 1970s. But as the Dutch had discovered, this would have resulted in the creation of enduring welfare expectations based upon a finite resource, and an agonising letdown when that resource had been exhausted. Alternatively – as the Labour Party argued – North Sea revenues could have been 'invested' directly by the state. But the whole history of state investment in Britain, from Concorde and launch-aid for the aerospace industry, through 'Plan for Coal' and steel investment in the middle 1970s, to the Humber Bridge and de Lorean, gave no grounds for optimism that such 'investment' would have produced a worthwhile return. By using oil revenues to shrink the budget deficit, and by abolishing controls on outward investment, the first Thatcher administration did what it could to ensure that the counterpart of those revenues would pass to genuinely productive long-term investment, whether at home or abroad, to generate future revenues long after North Sea oil has passed away. Our children will have cause to thank it for such prescience.

The accusation that the state has squandered the taxpayers' resources on riotous living – i.e. current spending – and allowed the nation's capital assets to decay is one that has been levelled at every government in recent years. It has indeed assumed the dimensions of a parrot cry – 'capital spending good, current spending bad'. As with most parrot cries, there is something in it. Departments and local authorities required to make economies do find it more convenient to take the axe to road, school or drainage programmes – so that the burden of adjustment falls upon the private sector – than to reduce the numbers they employ or to contain their wage costs. And there are incongruities to the way in which the national accounts are compiled. Private businesses do not lump the payroll and investment in new plant together for purposes of financing; nor is there any very obvious reason why investment by the Atomic

Energy Authority should be included in the calculation of the budget deficit, while investment by British Nuclear Fuels (also wholly state-owned) is not.

But the incongruities are not one-sided. Weapons procurement by the Ministry of Defence, for example, counts as current expenditure (on the grounds that they will never yield a commercial return). Besides, as already noted, the public sector makes many 'investments' which the private capital markets would have the good sense to leave well alone: it is, for example, hard to believe that a privatised British Rail would find many takers for investment in its electrification plans among those who had studied the productivity of its freight services. Nor is the Treasury's scepticism about the merits of market fund-raising 'outside the PSBR' by the nationalised industries as motiveless as it is usually chalked up to be. For unless the financial institutions which would have to produce the cash treated such fund-raising operations as analogous to a debenture from GEC or ICI, rather than in the same category as a conventional gilt issue, the PSBR is where they must belong.

A fairer charge against the Treasury is that the treatment it accords to sales of public assets conflicts with its own accounting principles. For if subscribers to a BR loan raised to modernise the London–Gatwick line would otherwise use their cash to buy gilts and help finance the budget deficit, then so might subscribers to the sale of a 49 per cent interest in British Aerospace. Yet asset sales are treated, not as an alternative method of financing the deficit, but as a method of reducing it. That is indeed illogical.

In the end, however, the only way to ensure that investment in the public corporations will be assessed on its commercial merits is by moving their ownership into the private sector – providing, that is, that any monopoly privileges they enjoy are, at the same time, dismantled. The sale of government shares in BP, or secondary issues of shares in Cable & Wireless, may be seen as no more than alternatives to the sale of gilts or National Savings, since these businesses are already assessed by private sector criteria. Selling shares in a legalised monopoly – British Gas or the CEGB, for example – would not achieve a true commercial judgement on their bids for funds since they would remain absolved from competition and require a regulatory supervision which would more logically be applied within the public sector. But for the most part the state-owned businesses disposed of between 1979 and 1983 – Amersham, British Aerospace, Britoil, Cable & Wireless at its original flotation, and (with reservations) Associated British Ports – were released to be judged by the markets on performance. That constituted a real 'rolling back of the frontiers of the state', and the first of any scale in our history.

The allegation that the abolition of exchange controls starved domestic industry of funds for investment hardly requires much refutation. As already pointed out, the retention of controls would have led inescapably to a greater 'overshoot' in the exchange rate in 1980/1, thereby further reducing the profitability of investment in British manufacturing industry. To the extent that British financial institutions would have remained locked in it is certainly arguable that the government would have been able to fund more cheaply: but that, one feels, would have been small consolation to the manufacturing sector which the opponents of exchange control liberalisation claimed to be so keen to help. As to the other side of the argument – that exchange controls prevented sterling being driven down by a tide of speculation – this always seemed an incongruous complaint from those who wanted to see a more 'competitive' exchange rate; but in any case it is entirely refuted by experience, which showed that exchange controls were power-less to prevent large-scale withdrawals of foreign-owned funds when they were in operation.

* * *

Inevitably the main ingredients in the balance-sheet of a modern British administration relate to economic perform-ance. There are, however, broader criticisms which have been levelled at the 1979 government which require considera-tion. It is said that in its international dealings it positively damaged long-term British interests by giving an appearance of insularity, selfishness and stridency; while at home it displayed an indifference verging on callousness towards the plight of the unemployed, the poor, the sick and the old, and widened inequalities and the 'North–South divide'.

That no British Prime Minister in living memory was less naturally attuned to the language of diplomacy than Mrs Thatcher may be readily conceded. The instinct to defend her corner is profound, and she has limited patience with those who lack a similar robustness of approach. Inevitably she viewed the Foreign Office with considerable suspicion: an attitude which was fully reciprocated. So long as Lord Carrington presided her impatience was contained. After his departure gloom descended.

Whether British interests were ill-served by the Prime Minister's combativeness is much more questionable. Over the Falklands affair, given the vociferousness – however narrowly based – of parliamentary resistance to compromise solutions, it is hard to believe that any Tory Prime Minister (and even questionably any Labour Prime Minister) would have risked successfully a different response to the Argentine invasion. Whether any other recent Tory Prime Minister would have seen that response through with such unflinching nerve is, of course, another matter.

In the arena where modern British diplomacy matters most – the European Community – the Prime Minister's fierce pursuit of what she saw as Britain's deserts dismayed the British diplomats and their attendant diplomatic correspondents. Yet she consistently secured her main objective of a large annual reimbursement of Britain's net contributions to the Community budget (so large, indeed, in 1981, that the account was almost put in balance). No doubt she made few friends in the process, although without a budget problem her relations with President Giscard d'Estaing could never have been cordial. But all experience suggests that genteel diplomacy could not have scored as highly in a circle where, for better or for worse, national self-assertiveness has usually paid the best dividends.

Yet budgetary refunds were at best a palliative, calculated only to make more bearable the extravagances and misdirected resources of the common agricultural policy. The goal of structural reform did not just elude Britain: it was never seriously attempted. The Ministry of Agriculture, never departmentally inclined to give much weight to the third part of its brief as Ministry of Food, entered with ill-disguised enthusiasm into the annual escalation of farmgate prices. The

Foreign Office clung to the repeatedly exposed illusion that the government of Bonn would prove a reliable ally in curbing agricultural spending, since the logical alternative of seeking common cause with France, which did not need exaggerated grain prices, as the Germans did, to satisfy a horde of weekend smallholders, was ruled out by historic jealousies between it and the Quai d'Orsay. Confronted by such powerful Whitehall currents, the Treasury became defeatist, settling for reinforcement of the Prime Minister's natural inclination to demand 'our money back'.

At the time of writing, the issue hangs in the balance. The Community needs extra funds to meet the endlessly spiralling cost of agricultural support and to cope with the recruitment of Spain and Portugal, Mrs Thatcher has served notice that she will veto those extra funds unless permanent arrangements are made to reduce the British budget share and to curb farm spending. The first condition looks unattainable – clubs do not usually offer country membership to city members. The second condition seems self-contradictory, since a proper curb to agricultural spending would eliminate the need for extra funds, while extra funds would postpone all prospect of a proper curb to agricultural spending. But the power to veto the allocation of extra funds is constitutionally unchallengeable; and if it is wielded unflinchingly the reform of farm pricing from which consumers throughout the Community stand to gain may yet be in Britain's grasp. If it is to be wielded unflinchingly the instincts of both the Foreign Office and the Ministry of Agriculture will have to be overridden. The risk remains considerable, therefore, that notwithstanding the Prime Minister's frequently-expressed distaste for 'fudged compromises', that is what will eventually emerge.

But if the first Thatcher administration pursued the lonely and ultimately self-defeating objective of budgetary relief, rather than the basic goal of more realistic farmgate prices, it was only following a hallowed tradition. The defeatism of Whitehall towards the common agricultural policy was entrenched in departmental attitudes, and successive postwar governments had almost invariably accepted without question the adversarial stance of British diplomacy towards the French who alone hold the key to ultimate reform.

In the context of relations with the world beyond the European Community the 1979 administration did distance itself to some extent from those that went before it. All previous postwar Prime Ministers, at any rate since Attlee, had seized the chance to bask in international limelight offered by the coming of jet travel with relish – sometimes even with obsession. Mrs Thatcher did not. She took no great pains to hide her impatience with the windy rhetoric of Western summitry and Commonwealth conferences; and hence incurred the wrath of those who continued to believe that heads of government put together can summon up a better world. In particular she stood accused of failure to 'give a lead' to concerted international action to cure the world recession.

Yet the evidence of positive performance from concerted summit action was flimsy, to put it at its best. It was alleged that in 1973, and again in 1978, the leading Western governments had consciously embarked on coordinated policies of expansion. The degree of conscious coordination was more apparent in retrospect than it had been at the time; and the 'oil shocks' which had rapidly ensued to bring expansion to a grinding halt were overlooked. So were the more numerous occasions when attempts to pick a 'locomotive' economy, or to advance in 'convoy', had collapsed in acrimony. At any rate it was the Prime Minister's settled conviction that fiscal and monetary self-discipline by the leading governments were the right priorities for the 1980s; and most of her international partners agreed with her. Indeed it was ironical that many of those who yearned for government-financed expansionism were also most critical of the irresponsibility of American deficit financing, and the magnetic attraction which it exerted on footloose funds to the detriment of other people's currencies.

Perhaps it was the 'tone' of the Thatcher Government which most united its critics in condemnation, from the Labour Party and the TUC through Liberals and SDP to the dissenters on the Tory benches, and embracing the academics, the salons and the majority of Fleet Street. Mrs Thatcher, it was said, had arrived in Downing Street proclaiming the prayer of St Francis ('Lord, make me an instrument of Your peace . . .') and, once installed, had stood the Sermon on the Mount upon its head.

Here again, that the 1979 administration marked a break

with the rhetoric of the past is undeniable. Throughout the postwar era 'compassion' had become a badge which politicians of all parties pinned upon their chests with pride. Labour Governments and their backbenchers claimed a monopoly of this virtue; Tories responded with the claim that through more efficient business management they would have more of it to spread around. Almost no one paused to reflect that compassion is supposed to be a personal characteristic, involving voluntary individual sacrifice on behalf of others less fortunately placed; whereas politicians who professed it were engaged in the imposition of sacrifices on the taxpayers at large, including, to an ever-increasing extent, the supposed beneficiaries.

As a result market criteria had been increasingly distorted. Obligations were imposed on businesses to observe externally-imposed wage rates, to locate their factories in problem areas, to buy off the depredations of health-and-safety-at-work inspectors, and to finance through rates and taxes a range and complexity of welfare services which mushroomed as their profitability and competitiveness shrank. Inevitably unemployment grew: governments hoped to escape the blame by reiterating their commitment to eliminate it, and their horror of the 'obscenity' that it represented while it lasted.

The 1979 administration took a different philosophical stance. Wealth had to be generated before it could be taxed; resources generated before they could be allocated to welfare. Unemployment reflected both the legacy of old bad habits and a swiftly changing environment. Government could and should soften the shock; it could not prevent it happening, and the spectacle of politicians tearing out their hair about it invited merited contumely. There *was* an emphasis on rewards and inequality; but it is a sadly inescapable consequence of the elimination of confiscatory rates of taxation on high incomes that high income-earners will benefit disproportionately.

There was thus a shift of emphasis, in emotive terms, from the halt to the healthy, based upon the proposition that the healthy were approaching the point at which they might prefer to stay at home. The invocation of the spirit – if not the name – of the scribe of Victorian self-reliance, Mr Samuel Smiles, wrinkled the noses of Belgravia. It does not seem to have done the government as much harm as the critics regularly expected in the grassroots.

Where the government *was* more vulnerable to criticism was in its failure to tackle some of the middle-class tax privileges which might have been justifiable in an era of confiscatory taxation and legalised control of salaries, but which were left as incongruities when those features were stripped away. Sir Geoffrey Howe did, it is true, indicate an intention to bring the whole range of 'perks' more comprehensively and equitably within the tax net following the slashing of the higher rates of tax in his 1979 Budget. Tory MPs were flooded with indignant protests and the idea was swiftly dropped. Similarly attempts to tax effectively the commonest perk, the company car, were consistently defeated by the dependence of the UK car industry on that sheltered market – and the sensitivities of its own supporters.

Most incongruous of all was the tolerance of massive diversion of the benefit of mortgage interest relief. By the summer of 1983 the Bank of England calculated that home-owners were taking out equity in their homes by borrowing on mortgage and using the proceeds to finance other purchases to the tune of £7000m a year. Yet the last of Sir Geoffrey Howe's Budgets raised the ceiling on relief from £25 000 to £30 000. Not only were home-owners given the exclusive ability to claim Exchequer aid for German cars and holidays in Spain; the task of monetary control was rendered far more difficult (and interest rates were arguably pushed or held higher than they would have been without the relief), and house prices were artificially inflated against the first-time home-buyer – the very people for whom the concession was supposedly designed. Such is the political muscle-power of home-ownership!

But perhaps the unkindest criticism of all those made against the first Thatcher administration (notably by Peter Riddell in *The Thatcher Government*) is the charge that its achievements came about through inadvertence and the *Zeitgeist*, and that only its failures were of its own contriving. Unemployment, social divisiveness, destruction of the country's industrial base: these were all primarily of the government's own doing. The dramatic fall in inflation, the surge in productivity, the shrinking incidence of industrial disputes, the recovery in managerial self-confidence: these, by contrast, were thrust upon us by the outside world. The first part of this charge has been dealt with; it is to the second that we must now turn.

Yet again, there is something to it. The capacity of governments to decide the destinies of nations has never been remotely commensurate with the ambitions of participants, and in modern Britain, a medium-sized economy exceptionally exposed to the international trading environment, it is little more than marginal for good or ill. The views of a New York stock market pundit such as Mr Henry Kaufman are liable to have a greater short-term impact on the course of British interest and exchange rates than all the best-laid plans of Great George Street; and a bunch of mullahs in the Persian Gulf can transform the whole business climate overnight.

The world recession brought about by two huge increases in the price of energy in 1973 and 1978–9, and the consequent transfer of revenue from advanced industrial countries with a high propensity to spend to a handful of Gulf oil states in no position to use at once and in full their new-found wealth, was the dominant influence on the British economy between 1979 and 1983. This influence was exacerbated by the dramatic jump in sterling between 1978 and 1981, for reasons which, as argued above, had not much to do with the policies of the British Government.

As a result fierce competition, at home and abroad, brought the hyperinflation of the 1970s to an abrupt end. Businesses confronted in the spring of 1980 with collapsing order-books (and in many cases still nursing searing memories of the financial traumas of late 1974) shed labour wholesale. Union militants discovered that their troops would no longer respond to orders. Managers, forced to fight and perform for survival, discovered they could do so.

Nor is it likely, judging by the French experience, that the espousal of the conventional neo-Keynesian response to recession would have made much enduring difference. The main beneficiaries would have been importers rather than home producers: that is why the critics who processed their alternative programmes of 'reflation' through the Treasury econometric model came out with little more than marginal improvements in the levels of domestic unemployment after five years.

So a major share of the credit (or blame – in the eyes of some) for the structural improvements in the performance of the British economy which occurred between 1979 and 1983 is not to be allocated to the Thatcher Government. But minor shares are not to be sneered at. Government action – and government refusal occasionally to act – also made a significant contribution.

There was the preparedness to accept historically exorbitant rates of interest in the autumn of 1979, as the economy moved into deep recession, in order to curb the growth of credit. Undoubtedly the transmission mechanism by which this contributed to the sharp fall in inflation from the summer of 1980 onwards – the soaring exchange rate for the pound – was not the one the government would have chosen. It had hoped that negotiators in the market place would read the signal, and adjust their bargains downwards in response. After all the years when governments had sought to accommodate escalating wage costs with currency depreciation, this was always too much to expect. But when the *force majeure* of currency appreciation materialised instead, the government did not flinch. On the contrary, in the spring of 1981 it flew in the face of all established postwar conduct by tightening the fiscal stance while the economy was still in deep recession.

At the time, in 1979 and 1980, Sir Geoffrey Howe was accused by many of the Government's admirers such as Professor Hayek of pursuing an excessively gradualist approach to inflation and thereby missing its opportunity; and by its far more numerous academic critics of monetarist dogmatism. In retrospect both criticisms look overstated. For at least the first twelve months of any new government the momentum of the economy is essentially the legacy of its predecessors. The strategy of the 1979 Budget may have been seriously flawed; but had it been word-perfect nothing could have averted a rapid escalation of both inflation and wage settlements. As for the charge of excessive rigidity, that is impossible to reconcile with the large permitted overshoot of the monetary targets in 1979 and 1980.

Politicians are regularly accused – with justice – of shortsightedness and impatience. Finding that the economy does not respond at once to their chosen strategy (because it cannot ever do so), they lose heart and nerve and change the strategy. Uniquely, the 1979 administration did not do so. Villified by the commentators and the academic establishment, increasingly unpopular in the country, increasingly questioned by its own backbenchers – not to mention the great producer lobbies of the CBI and TUC – it stuck grimly to its path. Not with inflexibility – it accepted a huge overshoot in the budget deficit in 1980/1 – but with determination. The 1981 Budget must rank as the most courageous in modern times. It enabled recovery from recession to take place without the reemergence of inflation. The 364 economists informed the readers of *The Times* it could not happen. Not for the first time, they were proved wrong.

Budgetary consistency was not enough. It was also essential that management should resume the responsibilities it had been stripped of by the futile exercises in centralised control of bargaining and prices in the 1960s and 1970s. Government consciously withdrew, to the profound discomfiture of union leaders who had looked forward with some relish to a repetition of the 'confrontations' that had marked, and ultimately destroyed, the 1970 Tory Government. It was a chequered progress, and there were still pitched battles with indecisive outcomes: the engineering strike of 1979, the steel strike of 1980, the civil service strike of 1981, the NHS disruption of 1982. Slowly but surely, however, the conventional assumption that union leadership with muscle and political motivation could always drive the government to fight on unfavourable terrain, and beat it, was shown to be without foundation. The changed environment could not have been more dramatically illustrated than by the contrast between the double rout inflicted by the miners on the government of 1970, and the triple failure of a dedicated left-wing miners' leader to bring his troops to battle in 1982–3.

Certainly the severity of the recession, and the consequential sense of insecurity, played the predominant role in this transformation. But it was of crucial importance that ordinary trades unionists should discover that they could defy the orders of fulltime shop stewards and get away with it. Sir Michael Edwardes at BL established a precedent in appealing to his work force to choose by secret ballot over the heads of the union apparat. It worked: others were swift to follow his example.

The Cassandras warn that this is not a lasting change. As unemployment begins to fall, and fear of the dole queue to recede, union solidarity will reassert itself, and do so with redoubled vigour to settle scores. We shall see. But it is not immediately obvious why employees who, throughout the 1960s and the 1970s, had been increasingly treated, by a union machinery to which they were often compulsorily attached, as strike fodder undeserving of consultation or consideration, should cheerfully surrender once again their new-found ability to make choices for themselves. At any rate the 1983 Annual Conference of the TUC, marked by an unprecedented outbreak of breast-beating about the failure of the rank and file to respond to orders and vote the Tories out, hardly suggested overweaning confidence that the Cassandras would prove right.

Courage and consistency may be admirable virtues in government: they are not usually deemed enough to bring home the electoral bacon. How are we to explain the Tories' landslide victory after four years in office? By almost every accepted yardstick of vote-winning performance, after all, Mrs Thatcher and her colleagues had a wretched tale to tell on 9 June 1983. For every ten men and women out of work when the nation had last polled in 1979, twenty-six now shared their plight. The economy had not grown in the interval, it had shrunk, and in the case of manufacturing output, shrunk dramatically. And instead of cutting taxes, as the Tory manifesto had pledged to do in 1979, the government had increased the total tax burden (including national insurance) on all except the well-to-do. Even the balance of payments, which in Harold Wilson's day had been treated – for reasons that were not immediately apparent – as a motive for electoral success was looking rocky. If ever there was a recipe for electoral disaster, this was it. Yet Mrs Thatcher secured the largest parliamentary majority since 1945. How could these things be?

Well, there was a divided and demoralised Opposition. The Tory share of the popular vote was actually smaller than it had been in 1979; but whereas in 1979 the anti-Tory vote had split 37 per cent to Labour and 19 per cent to the rest, in 1983 it had split right down the middle. The first-past-the-post electoral system then guaranteed a Tory landslide.

Mr Foot, for all his admirable personal qualities (indeed in part because of them) had proved the most disastrous leader thrown up by any major political party in recent experience. His party entered the 1983 election in a mood of deep despondency, which was rapidly confirmed as its convassers encountered suspicion and downright hostility on the doorstep even in its staunchest territories. Its plans for massive increases in public spending coupled with cuts in interest rates and indirect taxes and withdrawal from the Common Market were greeted with icy scepticism; while its programme of unilateral nuclear disarmament, which Mr Foot alone among its senior leaders fervently supported, was met with the accusation – from lifelong Labour supporters – that Labour had gone Communist.

But while this helps to explain the shift in votes from Labour to the Social Democrats and the Liberals, it does not begin to explain the remarkable stability in the Tory share of the total vote. Within that stability there were marked crosscurrents: the government, for example, won a much higher proportion of the first-time vote than it had in 1979. But on every previous occasion since the 1950s when third parties had prospered notably in General Elections – 1964, and twice in 1974 – the Tory Party had fallen victim. Not in 1983.

There was the 'Falklands factor'. After the long sad years of retreat from empire to a modest status in the international pecking order, the long-lingering memories of humiliation at Suez, and later on at the hands of de Gaulle and then domestic union bosses, the public responded almost with amazement to a government which had mounted singlehanded a most hazardous international military expedition, and brought it to triumphant fulfilment.

For all that, the Falklands were surely too remote from daily life on the council estates to provide an adequate explanation of the Tory landslide. But nearer home there was the spectacle of a government – the first for 20 years – which also proved capable of cutting the barons of the TUC down to size. The conventional wisdom of the 1960s and 1970s was that modern Britain was only governable in commission with the union leaders. Mrs Thatcher reckoned differently, and made her point. The 1983 election suggested that the mass of the electorate – indeed the mass of union members – viewed her performance in this respect with profound relief. When the election was fought and lost, the union leaders themselves, for the first time, began to concede the possibility that they had got it wrong.

There was also one particular policy initiative of the 1979 government which proved uniquely positive in swaying some key target votes: the legalised entitlement of council tenants to acquire their homes at a substantial discount on their market value. More than half a million citizens took advantage of this opportunity; but all the evidence suggests that its appeal went wider. And the political value of that appeal was reduplicated by the bitter opposition of the Labour Party and the active resistance of Labour-controlled local authorities. Here too, when the election was fought and lost, Labour prepared to bow to popular opinion: but here too it was by then too late.

There were, however, more fundamental trends at work than these. The discovery – well before the election was embarked upon – that the unemployed themselves were not prepared to attach much blame to the government for their plight came as a culture shock to Labour (and not only to Labour: the Alliance politicians and the Tory dissenters were almost equally scandalised). After all for 30 years and more, governments had avidly assumed responsibility for employment: yet here was a government presiding over levels of unemployment which we had all believed we would never see again, and no one seemed to blame it very much.

By the autumn of 1983, as the dust of the election began to settle, it was becoming fashionable to talk of Mrs Thatcher having 'changed the contours' of the British political battlefield. She had cast a spell, and fooled the electorate into accepting that ministers were powerless to control the economic waves. Perhaps the truth was a good deal more simple. Perhaps the public had long ago perceived that jobs could only be created and retained by behaviour and performance on the individual shopfloor, and instinctively responded to a government which dared to tell it as they saw it was, for a change.

But it is perhaps also true that the circumstances of unemployment had changed more than most observers had allowed for. Comparisons with the 1930s, when the redundancy notice was only separated by a matter of weeks from the soup-kitchen, had long been greatly overstated. But while the welfare state had removed the shadow of destitution from unemployment, it could not remove the social stigma. It sadly seemed to take a return to the levels of endemic unemployment of the 1930s to achieve that. Rapidly the embarrassment that had hitherto accompanied the acknowledgement of redundancy and worklessness diminished and disappeared.

That was not all. Throughout the postwar period British Governments had instinctively equated the interests of producers and consumers. The CBI, the TUC and the NFU: these were the voices that counted, and the fact that their corporate ambitions did not always or necessarily coincide with the self-interest of the majority of consumer-voters who were not affiliated to any of the three rarely occurred to ministers or officials except perhaps at election time. Under the 1979 government only the NFU retained its traditional influence intact – how fortunate it is for the NFU that ministers, including the Minister of Agriculture, are quite free to carry on as farmers, and in Tory Cabinets mostly do so. Otherwise Mrs Thatcher's instinct was to put the consumer first. No wonder the CBI was at one point driven to threaten her with a 'bare knuckle fist-fight'. It was an unprecedented demotion. But that it should apparently have been rewarded with electoral endorsement does not seem all that surprising. For the minority of us who are producers, the ability to win orders at rewarding prices must have first priority; and in the circumstances of 1979–83 that was often difficult, and not infrequently impossible. But for the totality of voters, who are all consumers, relative stability and predictability of price, and breadth of choice, are most important. The first Thatcher Government was the first in living memory to give priority to those goals, and to make real headway towards them: partly by good luck, no doubt; but partly by good management.

In an interview with *The Director* magazine in the autumn following the General Election, the Prime Minister described the nature of the political debate in Britain that she hoped to see in future as an argument about 'a different way of achieving the same objective . . . more like Democrats and Republicans' in the United States. Or Christian Democrats and Social Democrats in Germany, she might have added.

It is far too soon to assert with confidence that that will be the pattern of the future. The grassroots of the Labour Party – a sparse pasture, in all conscience – are still commanded by the caucuses of militancy. Mr Foot's chosen successor, Mr Neil Kinnock, is a leader in the Wilson mould, hungry for office and with no ideological hang-ups about the compromises that may be needed to achieve it. But the party that he leads does not look as if it is about to give him uncommitted followers. If, by the time the next election comes, the electorate is in a mood for change, and Mr Kinnock has contrived to tame the appearance (if hardly the intentions) of his party sufficiently, the lurch to the command economy for which the Marxists yearn could still be resumed.

But public alienation from the modern Labour Party now runs deep. It may well retain its hold on Scotland, the North and the Welsh valleys. Whether it can ever reestablish an effective grip on voting preferences south of the Tees and east of the Severn is much more problematical. The determination of the majority of the TUC to defy the catcalls of the Scargills and the Jenkinses and to seek a *modus vivendi* with the reelected Conservative Government, even at the cost of surrender of its right to circumscribe the options, is surely highly symptomatic. Labour's defeats in 1970 and 1979 did not shift the complacency of the union leadership about its ability to deliver its membership to a Labour Government, and to share the spoils. 1983 did.

Mrs Thatcher's vision of a future in which the electorate would be faced by a choice about means and not about ends is at least more believable today than it would have been at any time since the 1960s, and the failure of Hugh Gaitskell to move his party to a stance of Social Democracy. It is a huge prize. For Britain has been unique for too long among the advanced industrial economies in offering to its electorate as its alternative a government dominated by influences fundamentally opposed to a free economy. Even in countries such as France and Italy with large Communist parties, they have been successfully excluded from power, or neutered. In Britain alone they have regularly come within the gate. Maybe not again.

For the Tory Party it could prove a double-edged victory. For while the traditional Tory themes of continuity, good management, paternalism and opportunity will retain their appeal to the respectful and the ambitious, fear of what the alternative implies has become a powerful influence upon the floating voter. Mr Wedgwood Benn and Mr Scargill are formidable recruiting sergeants for the Tory Party. Dr Owen and Mr Steel are not. History's verdict on Mrs Thatcher could yet be that she saved the nation, and dished her party. It might be a verdict that all three deserved.

Index

189